W9-CUD-824

Chinese Characters
in
English Reading

Learning Chinese Characters (Hanzi) Through Your Native Language

— A New Way To Learn Chinese Characters (Hanzi) Visually

By

TAN JIMIN

谈 济民

(JIMMY TAN)
(WATANABE SAIMIN)

Chinese Character

JimmyTan's Hanzi · 汉 字

TanJimin method

CENGAGE
Learning™

Chinese Characters in English Reading
By Jimmy Tan

Re-printed in Tokyo 2023

汉字英读 · 漢字英読

Chinese Characters in English Reading

Learning Chinese Characters (Hanzi) Through Your Native Language
— A New Way To Learn Chinese Characters (Hanzi) Visually

by TAN JIMIN

谈 济 民

This is the first book in the world to write English and all other
languages with Chinese Characters (Hanzi), just like in Japanese.

English

For God so loved   the world,that he gave his only   begotten Son, that whosever
因r 神d 偌o 爱ved the 世ld, that 他e 给ve 他s 仅ly 生otten 子n, that   谁sever

believeth in   him should not perish, but have everlasting life.
信veth 于n 他m 应ld   不t 灭sh, 但t 有ve 永er续sting 命fe.

German

Denn also hat Gott die Welt geliebt, dass   er seinen eingeborenen Sohn gab,
因nn al偌o hat 神t die 世lt ge爱bt, dass 他r 他en   唯n生en   子n   给b,

auf dass alle, die an ihn glauben, nicht verloren werden, sondern das ewige Leben haben.
auf dass 全le, die 于n 他n 信en, 不t 失en 生en, 反rn das 永ge 命n 有ben.

French

Car Dieu a   tant aimé le monde qu'il a donné son Fils unique, afin que
因r 神u 有 偌nt 爱é le 世de qu'il a 给né 他n 子s 唯que, afin que

quiconque croit en lui ne périsse pas, mais qu'il ait la vie éternelle.
谁iconque 信t 于n 他i 不e 灭sse pas, 但s qu'il 有t la 命e 永le.

Spanish

Porque de tal   manera amó Dios al mundo, que ha dado a su Hijo unigénito,
因que de 偌l 形ra   爱ó 神 al 世do, que ha 给do a 他u 子o 唯生to,

para que todo aquel que en él cree, no se pierda, mas tenga vida eterna.
para que 全do aquel que 于n 他l 信e, 不o 自e 灭da,   但s 有ga 命da 永na.

Latin

Sic enim dilexit Deus mundum, ut Filium suum unigenitum daret; ut omnis qui
偌c 因m 爱exit 神s 世dum,   ut 子um 他m 唯生tum 给t; ut 全s 谁i

credit in eum, non pereat, sed habeat uitam aeternam.
信t 于n 他m, 不n 灭eat, 但d 有eat 命am 永nam.

Russian

Ибо так возлюбил Бог мир, что дал Сына Единородного, чтобы каждый
因o 偌к 爱бил 神г 宇р, что 给л 子на 唯но生го,   чтобы 皆дый

верующий в Него не   погиб, но имел жизнь вечную.
信щий 于 他го 不е по灭б, 但о 有л 命нь 永ую.

3

Preface

With the rapid development of Chinese economy and culture in recent years, China has become a country which attracts the world's attention. Not only the investors of every country come swarming into China, making China become the heaven of those pioneering men, but also those ordinary people in the world look at China with new eyes, flowing to travel and visit China. The European and American tourists who travel to China can amount to several tens of millions.

However, when walking on the streets in China, the tourists from eastern countries which have some relations with Chinese characters such as Japan, Korea and Vietnam, will be familiar with the signboards and road signs with Chinese characters on the street. Nevertheless, among those European and American tourists, over 99% of them are all in the fluster to the signs. Although they can sense a hint of oriental mystery, the meanings of those signboards are all Greek to them.

Mr. Tan, Jimin invents an easy way for westerners to recognize Chinese characters — a book named Chinese Characters in English Reading — An Easy Way to Visually Recognize Chinese Characters in English. So the westerners who never learn Chinese can also understand the meanings of the signboards and road signs as easily as visitors from Japan, Korea, and Vietnam, appreciating the witness of them.

This book doesn't require that the European and American readers must learn Chinese. Instead, some frequently used English phrases; interesting short essays and famous poetry are written in English mixed with some Chinese characters. Because the phrases are written in English mixed with some Chinese characters, they can read fluently in English, at the same time, they can know and memorize the meanings of some common Chinese characters.

This way is developed from the way of Japanese writing system, which is also adding some Chinese characters. Even if Japanese people can not understand Chinese language, they can recognize many Chinese characters, because they learn these characters when they write Japanese which includes some Chinese characters. Therefore, Japanese can easily know the meaning of signboards on the streets in China.

The visitors from western countries can learn many Chinese characters if they read this book before coming to China. Besides, the book introduces in detail about the strokes of Chinese characters, the witness in the Chinese four-character phrases, the evolution of these characters, interesting words and some Chinese characters appeared on the streets. If the westerners acquire some preparatory knowledge after reading this book, I believe they can feel closer to Chinese culture when they are walking on the Chinese streets.

It is a significant attempt to spread this way of recognizing Chinese characters to the world. Whether it will be successful is still under observation. It is of great importance for the Thomson Learning Company to present this book to the world. I hope after the book is published, the new way of recognizing Chinese can be improved consistently, being a mature and popular way for the people speaking any other language in the world.

It can be imagined that after the popularization of the knowledge of Chinese characters, westerners may write "十千 to 一" instead of long English phrase "ten thousands to one". Take another example, they may write "many 人 said" rather than "many people said", etc. This may be a novel way of communication between east and west in the future, which the book Chinese Characters in English Reading — An Easy Way to Visually Recognize Chinese Characters in English leads to.

By Xu, Baohua

·The former Executive Manager of the Linguistic Association of China.
·The professor of Fudan University, China.

2005.3.19

汉字英读，记忆神速

—When you read Chinese characters in English, you can remember them speedily.

Book Introductions

A

B

The above two books are the first two monographs in the field that revealed the close relationship between Chinese language and Indo-European languages including English, also written by TAN JIMIN, the author of this book.

A. ≪*The Approximation Discovery of Chinese-English Vocabulary Derivations*≫ was published in 2001 in Beijing. ISBN7-5022-2427-0/H313

B. ≪*A testimony of the language Affinity between Chinese & English* ≫ was published in 2006 in Taipei. ISBN957-549-663-9

Contents

Reading Hanzi

One.	They had only 一ne child.
Two.	In a day or 二o.
Three.	A child of 三e.
Four.	The hotel is 四r star.
Five.	A 五ve-year-old boy.
Six.	It is 六x of one and half a dozen of the other.
Seven.	The 七n wonders of the world.
Eight.	八t pages.
Nine.	九ne percent.
Ten.	I'd 十n times rather do that.

New Hanzi

一ne	one	六x	six
二o	two	七n	seven
三e	three	八t	eight
四r	four	九ne	nine
五ve	five	十n	ten

Reading Hanzi–Practice

① 三e times 二o is 六x.
② 四r and 四r makes 八t.
③ 五ve-and-十n-cent Store
④ Don't put the books at 六xes and 七ns.
⑤ the 七n deadly sins
⑥ in 九ne cases out of 十n
⑦ lesson 一ne
⑧ 一ne by 一ne
⑨ in 二os and 三es
⑩ 五ve-八t
⑪ 九ne days wonder

English Reading

① Three times two is six. ② Four and four makes eight.
③ Five-and-ten-cent Store ④ Don't put the books at sixes and sevens.
⑤ the seven deadly sins ⑥ in nine cases out of ten ⑦ lesson one
⑧ one by one ⑨ in twos and threes ⑩ Five-Eight ⑪ nine days wonder

Hanzi Colum

中 (center)

At first the character 中 (center) depicted a scene in which a flag was grasped by a hand in middle of it. Later, the flag, shown flapping in wind was eliminated, and only the flagpole and the hand remained, forming the character 中 (center).

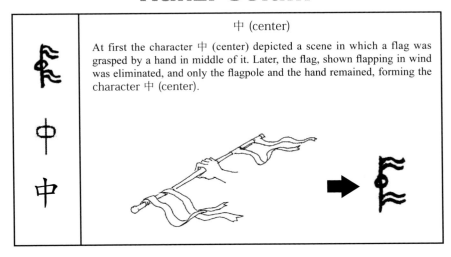

Writing Hanzi

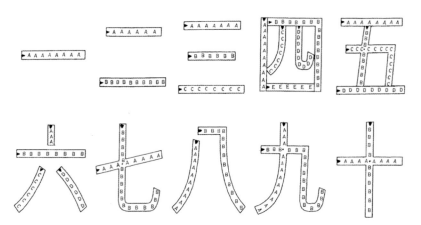

Proverb Wisdom

【三e 心ds 二o 意ghts】 (three · minds · two · thoughts)

☞ *with three minds and two opinions*

Explanation : have two minds about

Example : Don't treat your colleagues ***half-heartedly*** (→ *with three minds and two thoughts*).

【多s 此s 一ne 举n】 (surplus · this · one · action)

☞ *this is a surplus action*

Explanation : make an unnecessary move / burn daylight

Example : It is really ***an unnecessary move*** (→ *a surplus action*) in doing so.

Hanzi Combinations

【星期一】(star · circle · one) .... Monday

【星期二】(star · circle · two) .... Tuesday

【星期三】(star · circle · three) .... Wednsday

【星期四】(star · circle · four) .... Thursday

【星期五】(star · circle · five) .... Friday

【星期六】(star · circle · six) .... Saturday

【星期日】(star · circle · sun) .... Sunday

【一月】 (one · month / first · month)........................ January

【二月】 (two · month / second · month).................... February

【三月】 (three · month / third · month) .... March

Street Hanzi

★ 上海友谊商店 ＝ Shanghai Friendship Store

upper · sea	friend · feelings	trade · shop
上海	友谊	商店
Shanghai	Friendship	Store

Reading **H**anzi

一ne.   The streets were crowded with 人le.

二o.   Don't be a 儿d.

三e.   The thought 入ered his mind.

四r.   I have visited the town 几l times.

五ve.   to cut with a 刀fe

六x.   The patient is gathering 力th.

七n.   He was born with a silver 匕n in his mouth.

八t.   卜ne by tossing coins.

九ne.   a 厂y worker

十n.   He won't do that 又n.

New Hanzi

人le	people	刀fe	knife	厂y	factory
儿d	child	力th	strength	又n	again
入er	enter	匕n	spoon		
几l	several	卜ne	divine		

Reading Hanzi–Practice

① bear a 儿d
② the Chinese 人le
③ a 刀fe and fork
④ the 力th of mind
⑤ 匕n up soup
⑥ an iron 厂y
⑦ 几l 人le
⑧ this 儿d
⑨ 入er port

⑩ after 几l days
⑪ before you can say 刀fe
⑫ 入er the Army
⑬ enormous 力th
⑭ a 厂y girl
⑮ 卜ne by the 八t Trigrams
⑯ 又n and 又n
⑰ 卜ne by astrology
⑱ once 又n

English Reading

① bear a child ② the Chinese people ③ a knife and fork
④ the strength of mind ⑤ spoon up soup ⑥ an iron factory
⑦ several people ⑧ this child ⑨ enter port ⑩ after several days
⑪ before you can say knife ⑫ enter the Army ⑬ enormous strength
⑭ a factory girl ⑮ divine by the Eight Trigrams ⑯ again and again
⑰ divine by astrology ⑱ once again

Hanzi Colum

人 (person)

This is a typical hieroglyphic Chinese character. The Chinese character 人 (person) in the Jiaguwen* and Jinwen** eras was a sketch of a man standing while extending his hand. Later, the extended hand was removed leaving the present 人 (person). It shows a person with his legs spread, standing up.

* the Jiaguwen era: the inscription on bones or tortoise shells of the Shang Dynasty, B.C.1600 ~
** the Jinwen era: the inscriptions on ancient bronze objects, B.C.1100 ~

Writing Hanzi

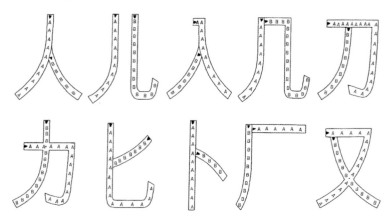

Proverb Wisdom

【暗k 箭w 伤t 人le】 (dark · arrow · hurt · people)

   ☞ *to hurt people with dark arrow*

   Explanation :   mill in the darkness

   Example   :   We must beware of those villains who *injure others by clandestine means* (→ *hurt people with dark arrow*).

【量re 力th 而d 行t】 (measure · strength · and · act)

   ☞ *to measure one's strength and act*

   Explanation :   do what one is capable of

   Example   :   In work and study, he always *acts according to his ability* (→ *measure his strength and act*) and never reaches for unattainable goal.

Hanzi Combinations

【人味】 (people · smell / (man · smell)) .... humanness
【儿科】 (child · branch) .... pediatrics
【入神】 (enter · spirit) .... entranced
【几何】 (several · how) .... geomatry
【刀鱼】 (knife · fish / (sword · fish)) .... hairtail
【力学】 (strength · study / (strength · learning)) .... mechanics
【匕首】 (spoon · head) .... dagger
【造船厂】(make · ship · factory) .... shipyard
【又及】 (again · reach) .... postscript (PS)

Street Hanzi

★ 平凉路第四小学 ＝ Flat-Cool Road No.4 Primary School

flat · cool	road	No. · four	little · learn
平凉	路	第四	小学
Flat-Cool	Road	No.4	Primary School

15

UNIT 3

Reading Hanzi

一 ne.   The children were play at 士 ers.

二 o.   He died on Irish 土 l.

三 e.   This machine can do the 工 k of ten men.

四 r.   Don't move an 寸 ch.

五 ve.   His children are 大 g now.

六 x.   It's 小 l of you not to answer his letter.

七 n.   I have six 口 ths to feed.

八 t.   山 t Everest is the highest mountain in the world.

九 ne.   She is wearing a 巾 f.

十 n.   We'll have a party this 夕 ng.

New Hanzi

士 er	soldier	大 g	big	巾 f	scarf
土 l	soil	小 l	small	夕 ng	evening
工 k	work	口 th	mouth		
寸 ch	inch	山 t	mount		

16

Reading Hanzi–Practice

① become a 土er
② a private 土er
③ till the 土l
④ rich 土l
⑤ looking for 工k
⑥ sloppy 工k
⑦ 寸ch by 寸ch
⑧ The car missed my dog by 寸ches.
⑨ 大g toe
⑩ the 大g bang
⑪ a 小l house
⑫ live on a 小l income
⑬ Shut your 口th!
⑭ the 口th of a bottle
⑮ 山t Tai
⑯ 山t Fuji
⑰ piano 巾f
⑱ good 夕ng
⑲ the 夕ng star
⑳ the 夕ng meal

English Reading

① become a soldier ② a private soldier ③ till the soil ④ rich soil
⑤ looking for work ⑥ sloppy work ⑦ inch by inch
⑧ The car missed my dog by inches. ⑨ big toe ⑩ the big bang
⑪ a small house ⑫ live on a small income ⑬ Shut your mouth!
⑭ the mouth of a bottle ⑮ Mount Tai ⑯ Mount Fuji ⑰ piano scarf
⑱ good evening ⑲ the evening star ⑳ the evening meal

Hanzi Colum

山 (mountain)

This is a typical hieroglyphic Chinese character. The character 山 (mountain) in the Jiaguwen era showed three mountains of the same height, but later the middle one was lengthened and the character 山 (mountain) was formed.

Writing Hanzi

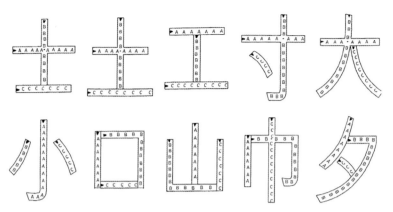

Proverb Wisdom

【口th 是ght 心t 非ng】 (mouth · right · heart · wrong)

☞ *to be right with the mouth and wrong at heart*

Explanation : cry with one eye and laugh with the other

Example : Your friend *cries with one eye and laughs with the other* (→ *is right with the mouth and wrong at heart*).

【铁n 证ce 如ke 山n】 (iron · evidence · like · mountain)

☞ *ironclad evidence can't explode like a mountain*

Explanation : irrefutable evidence

Example : Take the axe with you. It's *cast-iron evidence* (→ *ironclad evidence can't be explode like a mountain*), he can't deny it.

Hanzi Combinations

【士气】(soldier · airs / (soldier · spirit)) .... morale
【土豆】(soil · bean) .... potato
【工本】(work · root) .... cost
【尺寸】(foot · inch) .... size
【大小】(large · small) .... size
【大大】(large · large) .... greatly
【口齿】(mouth · tooth) .... enunciation
【山羊】(mountain · sheep) .... goat
【毛巾】(hair · kerchief) .... towel

Street Hanzi

★ 健康活泼 = Healthful and Lively
★ 嫩江路幼儿园 = Tender River Road Kindergarten

health · well-being	lively · pungent	tender · river	road	young · child · garden
健康	活泼	嫩江	路	幼儿园
healthful	lively	Tender River	road	kindergarten

UNIT 4

Reading Hanzi

一ne.　Her eyes were 广de with surprise.

二o.　The 门r is ajar.

三e.　Don't be afraid! It's just a 尸se.

四r.　Shoot an arrow from a 弓w.

五ve.　I have a 子n, but no 女er.

六x.　She is a teenage 女l.

七n.　You can lead a 马se to water but you can't make it drink.

八t.　He became 王ng of England.

九ne.　The house is made of 木d.

十n.　A barking 犬g seldom bites.

New Hanzi

广de	wide	子n	son	王ng	king
门r	door	女er	daughter	木d	wood
尸se	corpse	女l	girl	犬g	dog
弓w	bow	马se	horse		

20

Reading Hanzi–Practice

① 广de of the mark
② the 广de ocean
③ Remember to lock the 门r.
④ a wooden 门r
⑤ a living 尸se
⑥ draw a 弓w
⑦ a 弓w and arrow
⑧ an only 子n
⑨ a 女l friend
⑩ 女l Friday

⑪ a 马se of different color
⑫ ride a 马se
⑬ an oil 王ng
⑭ the 王ng of 王ngs
⑮ 王ng Lear
⑯ 木d carving
⑰ 木d nymph
⑱ a guide 犬g
⑲ Let sleeping 犬gs lie.

English Reading

① wide of the mark ② the wide ocean ③ Remember to lock the door.
④ a wooden door ⑤ a living corpse ⑥ draw a bow ⑦ a bow and arrow
⑧ an only son ⑨ a girl friend ⑩ girl Friday ⑪ a horse of different color
⑫ ride a horse ⑬ an oil king ⑭ the king of kings ⑮ King Lear
⑯ wood carving ⑰ wood nymph ⑱ a guide dog ⑲ Let sleeping dogs lie.

Hanzi Colum

木 (wood)

This is a typical hieroglyphic Chinese character. Presently the character 木 means wood or lumber, but originally it meant tree. In the Jiaguwen era the upper half of the character shows the branches of a tree, and the lower half shows its roots. In order to make it easier to write, the branches in the top part were changed into a cross with a horizontal and a vertical line.

Writing **H**anzi

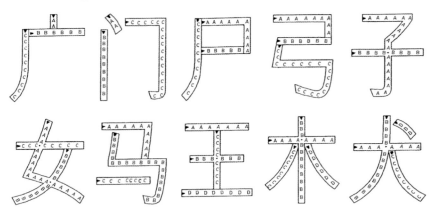

Proverb Wisdom

【鸡n 犬g 不t 宁l】 (chicken · dog · not · tranquil)

☞ *even the chickens and dogs can't be tranquil*

Explanation : even the fowls and dogs are not left in peace

Example : Smith scolded his wife, then scolded his children. He stirred the whole family *into a tempest* (→ *even the chickens and dogs can't be tranquil*).

【开n 门r 见e 山n】 (open · door · see · mountain)

☞ *to open the door and see the mountain in front*

Explanation : declare one's intention immediately

Example : You'd better *come straight to the point* (→ *open the door and see the mountain in front*). Don't beat about the bush.

Hanzi Combinations

【广告】(widely · inform) .... advertisement
【门牌】(door · plate) .... house number plate
【子宫】(child · palace) .... uterus, womb
【女皇】(woman · emperor) .... empress
【女王】(woman · king) .... queen
【马虎】(horse · tiger) .... careless, casual
【马上】(horse · up) .... immediately, at once
【木石】(wood · stone) .... a lifeless thing, a senseless being
【木星】(wood · star) .... Jupiter
【后门】(after · door / (back · door)) .... influence, back door

Street Hanzi

★ 兄弟面馆 ＝ Brothers Noodle House

elder brother · younger brother　　　noodle · house
兄弟　　　　　　　　　　　　　面馆
Brothers　　　　　　　　　　　Noodle House

23

Reading Hanzi

一ne.   He took me for a drive in his 车r.

二o.   The 戈xe is an Chinese ancient weapon.

三e.   A 瓦le was blown off the roof during the typhoon.

四r.   The earth moves around the 日n.

五ve.   The children gathered 贝ls on the beach.

六x.   I like to dive in the 水er.

七n.   Can you 见e the tower over there?

八t.   I saw an 牛x pulling a cart.

九ne.   She suddenly took my 手d and grasped it.

十n.   We import large quantities of 毛l from Australia.

New Hanzi

车r	car	贝l	shell	手d	hand
戈xe	dagger-axe	水er	water	毛l	wool
瓦le	tile	见e	see		
日n	sun	牛x	ox		

Reading Hanzi-Practice

① 车r wash
② go in a 车r
③ Have a 瓦le loose.
④ be on the 瓦les
⑤ a place in the 日n
⑥ under the 日n
⑦ Come out of your 贝l !
⑧ draw into his 贝l
⑨ 水er bird
⑩ 水er Gate
⑪ I'll 见e.
⑫ Let me 见e.
⑬ I 见w a picture on the wall.
⑭ I 见w him cross the street.
⑮ 牛x bow
⑯ 牛xford University
⑰ change 手ds
⑱ 手ds off!
⑲ Keep your 毛l on.
⑳ wear 毛l

English Reading

① car wash ② go in a car ③ Have a tile loose. ④ be on the tiles
⑤ a place in the sun ⑥ under the sun ⑦ Come out of your shell!
⑧ draw into his shell ⑨ water bird ⑩ Water Gate ⑪ I'll see. ⑫ Let me see.
⑬ I saw a picture on the wall. ⑭ I saw him cross the street. ⑮ ox bow
⑯ Oxford University ⑰ change hands ⑱ Hands off! ⑲ Keep your wool on.
⑳ wear wool

Hanzi Colum

水 (water)

This is a typical hieroglyphic Chinese character. The middle curved line depicted the flow of the river, and the points on each side depicted the waves and spray of the river. These side points later became longer curved lines, the middle curved line was straightened, forming the present character 水 (water).

Writing Hanzi

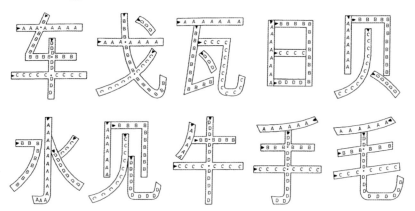

Proverb Wisdom

【大ly 显y 身y 手d】 (greatly · display · body · hand)

☞ *greatly display one's body and hand*

Explanation : display one's talents to the full

Example　　: A teacher should give his students many chances to **display fully their talents** (→ *greatly display their body and hand*).

【滴p 水er 穿ce 石ne】 (drop · water · pierce · stone)

☞ *dropping water can pierce the stone*

Explanation : constant dropping wears away a stone

Example　　: A full-length novel takes a long time to read, but **small strokes fell great oaks** (→ *dropping water can pierce the stone*).

Hanzi Combinations

【车床】(car · bed) .... lathe
【车站】(car · stand) .... station, bus stop
【干戈】(offend · dagger-axe) .... war
【日本】(sun · root) .... Japan
【日记】(daily · record) .... diary
【水晶】(water · glittering) .... crystal, rock crystal
【见闻】(see · listen) .... knowlege
【吹牛】(blow · ox) .... boast, brag, talk-big
【手法】(hand · method) .... skill, technique
【毛重】(hair · weight) .... gross-weight

Street Hanzi

★ 三田洋品店 ＝ Three-Fields Western Goods Shop

three · field	ocean · product	shop
三田	洋品	店
Three-Fields	Western Goods	shop

UNIT 6

Reading Hanzi

一ne.　　Air is made up of oxygen and other 气ses.

二o.　　I want to eat another 片ce of cake.

三e.　　one 斤m

四r.　　The cat scratched the furniture with its 爪ws.

五ve.　　Jean Henri Dunant was the 父er of the Red Cross.

六x.　　The 月n is shining brightly tonight.

七n.　　I 欠we my uncle $100.

八t.　　The leaves came whirling down in the 风d.

九ne.　　He has great 文y skill.

十n.　　This is a 方re board.

New Hanzi

气s	gas	父er	father	文y	literary
片ce	piece	月n	moon	方re	square
斤m	kilogram (kg)	欠w	owe		
爪w	claw	风d	wind		

Reading Hanzi–Practice

① 气s heater
② 气s mask
③ cut a pie into six 片ces
④ a 片ce of machinary
⑤ two 斤ms
⑥ 爪w hammer
⑦ 父er figure
⑧ 父er Time
⑨ howl at the 月n
⑩ promise a person the 月n
⑪ I 欠we 3 month's rent.
⑫ I 欠we him an apology.
⑬ break 风d
⑭ See how the 风d blows.
⑮ 文y language
⑯ 文y works
⑰ a 方re of cloth
⑱ The 方re of three is nine.

English Reading

① gas heater ② gas mask ③ cut a pie into six pieces ④ a piece of machinery
⑤ two kilograms ⑥ claw hammer ⑦ father figure ⑧ Father Time
⑨ howl at the moon ⑩ promise a person the moon ⑪ I owe 3 month's rent.
⑫ I owe him an apology. ⑬ break wind ⑭ See how the wind blows.
⑮ literary language ⑯ literary works ⑰ a square of cloth
⑱ The square of three is nine.

Hanzi Colum

月 (moon)

During the Jiaguwen era, the moon was in the form of a new moon (夕) which climbed the night sky. Since the moon always appears in the evening sky, this character was also used to mean evening. Considerably later, a horizontal line was added to the middle of the shape and the character 月 (moon) was formed.

Writing **H**anzi

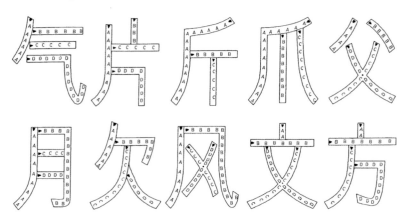

Proverb Wisdom

【捕tch 风d 捉tch 影w】 (catch · wind · clutch · shadow)

☞ *to catch the winds and clutch the shadows*

Explanation : chase the wind and clutch at shadows

Example : He likes *to make groundless accusations* (→ *to catch the winds and clutch the shadows*). Don't believe him.

【乘de 风d 破k 浪ve】 (ride · wind · break · wave)

☞ *to ride the wind and break the waves*

Explanation : brave the wind and the waves

Example : The police *ride the wind and break the waves* (→ *to ride the wind and break the waves*) to arrest smugglers at sea.

Hanzi Combinations

【气象】(air · appearance) .... meteorology
【影片】(shadow · piece) .... movie
【爪牙】(talon · tooth / (talon · fang)) .... lackey, underling
【月经】(monthly · pass) .... menstruation
【月老】(moon · elder / (The Old Man of Moon) .... matchmaker
【欠揍】(lack · beat) .... need a spanking
【风水】(wind · water) .... geomantic omen
【风流】(wind · flow) .... romantic
【文化】(literary · convert) .... civilization
【方正】(square · straight) .... upright, righteous

Street Hanzi

★ 人民大道 = the People's Main Road

person · people   large · road
人民   大道
People's   Main Road

Reading Hanzi

一ne.　Most animals are afraid of 火re.

二o.　The trapped fox 斗led violently to get free.

三e.　The 户d was still asleep at six in the morning.

四r.　Her 心t sank.

五ve.　示w your ID card, please.

六x.　to kill two birds with one 石ne

七n.　A 龙n is an imaginary animal.

八t.　Can we see the star with the naked 目ye?

九ne.　The old man is still working in his 田d.

十n.　They clear away the 皿shes.

New Hanzi

火re	fire	示w	show	田d	field
斗le	struggle	石ne	stone	皿sh	dish
户d	household	龙n	dragon		
心t	heart	目ye	eye		

Reading Hanzi–Practice

① play with 火re
② set the world on 火re
③ the 斗le for existence
④ 斗le against
⑤ 户d word
⑥ the 户d Cavalry
⑦ 心t and soul
⑧ lose 心t
⑨ 示w a person the door
⑩ 示w the bill
⑪ a 石ne wall
⑫ a 心t of 石ne
⑬ 龙n Well Tea
⑭ 龙n boat
⑮ see 目ye to 目ye
⑯ under a person's 目yes
⑰ 田d sports
⑱ 田d trip
⑲ the main 皿sh
⑳ 皿sh towel

English Reading

① play with fire ② set the world on fire ③ the struggle for existence
④ struggle against ⑤ household word ⑥ the Household Cavalry
⑦ heart and soul ⑧ lose heart ⑨ show a person the door ⑩ show the bill
⑪ a stone wall ⑫ a heart of stone ⑬ Dragon Well Tea ⑭ dragon boat
⑮ see eye to eye ⑯ under a person's eyes ⑰ field sports ⑱ field trip
⑲ the main dish ⑳ dish towel

Hanzi Colum

田 (field)

This is a typical hieroglyphic Chinese character. During the Jiaguwen era, the character consisted of five, seven or more fields, not limited to four fields like the present character 田 (field). Sometimes it consisted of even more than 12 fields, and was one of the most troublesome pictograms to write! During the Jinwen era, it was simplified to four rice fields.

Writing Hanzi

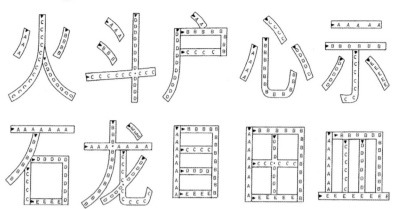

Proverb Wisdom

【归ning 心t 似ke 箭w】 (returning · heart · like · arrow)

☞ *the heart want to return just like a flying arrow*

Explanation : with one's heart set on speeding home

Example   : The two brothers were walking quickly, their ***hearts set on speeding home*** (→ *hearts want to return just like an flying arrow*).

【目ye 不t 识w 丁be】 (eye · not · know · cube)

☞ *one's eye don't know the cube / note : the character ' 丁 be' (cube) is most simple one in Chinese characters.*

Explanation : be totally illiterate

Example   : Having had little schooling, ***he did not know his ABCs*** (→ *his eyes don't know the cube*).

Hanzi Combinations

【火车】	(fire · car)	train
【火花】	(fire · flower)	spark
【火山】	(fire · mountain)	volcano
【火星】	(fire · star)	Mars
【火药】	(fire · medicine)	gunpowder
【火葬】	(fire · funeral)	cremation
【斗嘴】	(struggle · mouth)	quarrel
【粗心】	(thick · heart)	careless
【细心】	(thin · heart)	careful, attentive
【心肝】	(heart · liver)	darling, dear, honey
【心急】	(heart · fast)	impatient, short-tempered
【心焦】	(heart · charred)	anxious, worried
【示威】	(show · might)	demonstration
【石灰】	(stone · ash)	lime
【石棉】	(stone · cotton)	asbestos
【石油】	(stone · oil)	petroleum
【龙卷风】	(dragon · rolled · wind)	tornado
【龙头】	(dragon · head)	tap, faucet
【目前】	(eye · front)	at present
【田鸡】	(field · chiken)	frog
【田径】	(field · track)	athletics

Street Hanzi

★ 上海磁浮列车
= Shanghai Maglev Train

upper · sea	magnet · float	row · car
上海	磁浮	列车
Shanghai	Maglev	Train

35

Reading **H**anzi

一ne.　　The bird wore 白te feathers.

二o.　　water-瓜n

三e.　　The early 鸟d catches the worm.

四r.　　立d still, or I can't take your picture.

五ve.　　A square peg in a round 穴le.

六x.　　The purse is made of crocodile 皮n.

七n.　　grind 谷n into flour

八t.　　Necessity is the 母er of invention.

九ne.　　How 老d are you?

十n.　　He whispered in her 耳r.

New Hanzi

白te	white	穴le	hole	老d	old
瓜n	melon	皮n	skin	耳r	ear
鸟d	bird	谷n	grain		
立d	stand	母er	mother		

Reading Hanzi-Practice

① 白te bear
② 白te book
③ 瓜n
④ musk瓜n
⑤ 鸟ds of a feather flock together.
⑥ A little 鸟d told me.
⑦ 立d alone
⑧ 立d a chance
⑨ every 穴le and corner
⑩ a mouse 穴le
⑪ fair 皮n
⑫ have a thin 皮n
⑬ 母er tongue
⑭ 母er wit
⑮ 老d wine
⑯ an 老d custom
⑰ fall on deaf 耳rs
⑱ 耳r pick
⑲ 谷n elevator
⑳ a 田d of 谷n

English Reading

① white bear ② white book ③ melon ④ muskmelon
⑤ Birds of a feather flock together. ⑥ A little bird told me. ⑦ stand alone
⑧ stand a chance ⑨ every hole and corner ⑩ a mouse hole
⑪ fair skin ⑫ have a thin skin ⑬ mother tongue ⑭ mother wit
⑮ old wine ⑯ an old custom ⑰ fall on deaf ears ⑱ ear pick
⑲ grain elevator ⑳ a field of grain

Hanzi Colum

母 (mother)

This pictogram depicts a woman of mature age kneeling. A pair of breasts can be imagined dots on her chest. The character 母 (mother) was developed by attaching two dots (breasts) to the character 女 (woman) in the Jiaguwen age. Later, the character 女 (woman) became rectangular, and the breasts which were once arranged left and right, were moved to the top and bottom.

Writing **H**anzi

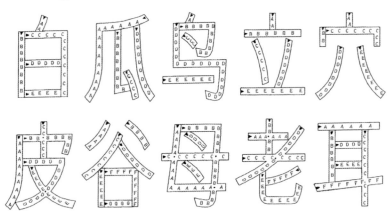

Proverb Wisdom

【隔n 墙l 有ve 耳r】 (partition · wall · have · ear)

☞ *on the other side of the partition wall there is a ear*

Explanation : walls have ears

Example   : "Not so loud" he warned her , afraid that they might be overheard, *"walls have ears"* (→ *on the other side of the partition wall there is a ear*).

【鹤ne 立d 鸡n 群p】 (crane · stand · chicken · group)

☞ *a crane stands among a group of chicken*

Explanation : a giant among dwarfs

Example   : Jack has achieved much and is like *a flower of the flock* (→ *a crane stands among chicken group*) in linguistic circles.

Hanzi Combinations

【老板】　(old · board) .... boss, shopkeeper
【老大】　(old · large) .... number one
【老天爷!】(old · sky · grandpa) .... My goodness!
【老光眼】(old · light · eye) .... presbyopia
【老花】　(old · flower) .... presbyopic
【白宫】　(white · palace) .... White　House
【白金】　(white · gold) .... platinum
【白木耳】(white · wood · ear) .... tremella
【立正!】(stand · straight) .... Attention!

Street Hanzi

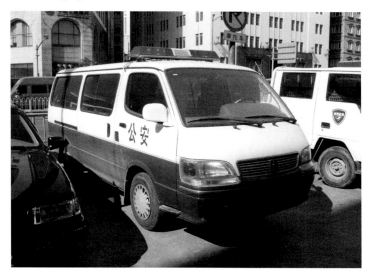

★ 公安 ＝ Public Security

public · ease
公安
Public Security

Reading Hanzi

一ne.　　The sun sets in the 西st.

二o.　　Open your books at 页ge 9.

三e.　　Even a 虫m will turn.

四r.　　The hot soup burned my 舌gue.

五ve.　　竹o ends and wood shavings all have their uses.

六x.　　臼r and pestle.

七n.　　She put her whole 己f into the job.

八t.　　Many soldiers shed 血d in the battle.

九ne.　　Fine 衣s make the man.

十n.　　We keep more than thousand 羊p.

New Hanzi

西t	west	竹o	bamboo	衣s	clothes
页ge	page	臼r	mortar	羊p	sheep
虫m	worm	己f	self		
舌gue	tongue	血d	blood		

Reading Hanzi–Practice

① 西t Point
② the 西t end
③ the sports 页ge
④ town 页ge
⑤ the 虫m of conscience
⑥ 虫m gear
⑦ set 舌gues wagging
⑧ 舌gue twister
⑨ 竹o shoots
⑩ 竹o leaf
⑪ crush in a 臼r
⑫ 己lf-control
⑬ 己lf-centered
⑭ in cold 血d
⑮ 血d is thicker than water.
⑯ 衣s tree
⑰ a suit of 衣s
⑱ a flock of 羊p
⑲ follow like 羊p

English Reading

① West Point ② the west end ③ the sports page ④ town page
⑤ the worm of conscience ⑥ worm gear ⑦ set tongues wagging
⑧ tongue twister ⑨ bamboo shoots ⑩ bamboo leaf ⑪ crush in a mortar
⑫ self-control ⑬ self-centered ⑭ in cold blood
⑮ Blood is thicker than water.
⑯ clothes tree ⑰ a suit of clothes ⑱ a flock of sheep ⑲ follow like sheep

Hanzi Colum

衣 (clothes)

The original meaning of the Chinese character 衣 (clothes) is coat, and the form of the character 衣 (clothes) is a depiction of the form of a coat.

Writing Hanzi

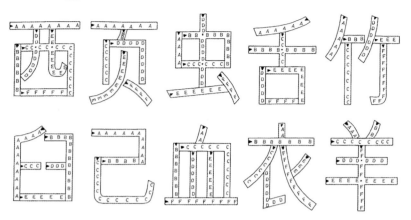

Proverb Wisdom

【成shed 竹o 在t 胸st】 (accomplished · bamboo · at · chest)

☞ *imagine an accomplished bamboo at one's chest*

Explanation : have one's cards up one's sleeves / have a well-thought-out plan

Example : The coach has *a well-thought-out plan* (→ *an imagine of an accomplished bamboo at his chest*) for tommorow's match.

【心t 血d 来me 潮de】 (heart · blood · come · tide)

☞ *one's heart blood comes tide*

Explanation : be seized by a whim

Example : *She has a whim* (→ *Her heart blood comes a tide*) for gardening, but it won't last long.

Hanzi Combinations

【虫齿】　(worm · tooth) .... decayed tooth
【舌战】　(tongue · battle) .... a verbal battle
【血汗钱】(blood · sweat · money) .... money earned by hard toil
【臼齿】　(mortar · tooth) .... molar
【页边】　(page · edge) .... margin

Street Hanzi

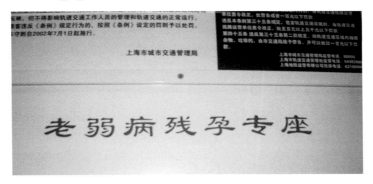

★ 老弱病残孕专座 = Special seat for the old, weak, sick, disabled and pregnant

old · weak · sick · disabled · pregnant   special · seat
老　弱　病　残　　孕   专座
the old, weak, sick, disabled and pregnant   special seat

UNIT 10

Reading Hanzi

一ne.　　We have a good crop of 米ce this year.

二o.　　Fine 羽ers make fine birds.

三e.　　I broke a 骨ne in my ankle while playing soccer.

四r.　　Beer and whisky are made from 麦y.

五ve.　　My baby can already 走k.

六x.　　Jack and the 豆n stalk

七n.　　I walked with a light 足t.

八t.　　Don't go out in the 雨n.

九ne.　　I had a 牙th removed at the dentist.

十n.　　Some people eat 鱼sh on Fridays.

New Hanzi

米ce	rice	走k	walk	牙th	tooth
羽er	feather	豆n	bean	鱼sh	fish
骨ne	bone	足t	foot		
麦y	barley	雨n	rain		

Reading Hanzi-Practice

① boil 米ce
② 米ce cake
③ birds of a 羽er
④ show the white 羽er
⑤ make old 骨nes
⑥ no 骨nes broken
⑦ 麦y wine
⑧ 麦y sugar
⑨ 走k of life
⑩ 走k a person off his feet
⑪ 豆n curd

⑫ coffee 豆n
⑬ have cold 足et
⑭ my 足t
⑮ sweep a person off his 足et
⑯ 雨n or shine
⑰ 雨n check
⑱ a permanent 牙th
⑲ in the 牙th of
⑳ Brush your 牙eth more carefully!
㉑ fried 鱼sh
㉒ drink like a 鱼sh

English Reading

① boil rice ② rice cake ③ birds of a feather ④ show the white feather
⑤ make old bones ⑥ no bones broken ⑦ barley wine ⑧ barley sugar
⑨ walk of life ⑩ walk a person off his feet ⑪ bean curd ⑫ coffee bean
⑬ have cold feet ⑭ my foot ⑮ sweep a person off his feet
⑯ rain or shine ⑰ rain check ⑱ a permanent tooth ⑲ in the tooth of
⑳ Brush your teeth more carefully! ㉑ fried fish ㉒ drink like a fish

Hanzi Colum

一三五 (one three five)

The Chinese character 一 (one) consists of one horizontal line, unchanged since the Jiaguwen era. It is probably the only character that has remained unchanged since that time. Since the Jiaguwen era, the characters one, two, three, and four were indicated entirely by horizontal lines (later the number four became 四).

From five up, the number of horizontal lines becomes inconvenient to write. The number five was depicted as X. Afterwards, horizontal lines were added to the top and bottom of X, and the X was changed to finally form the present 五 (five).

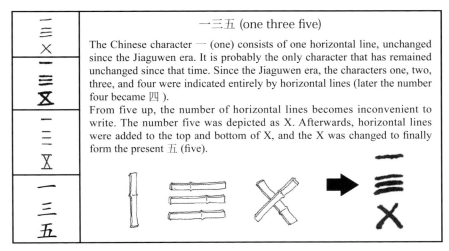

Writing Hanzi

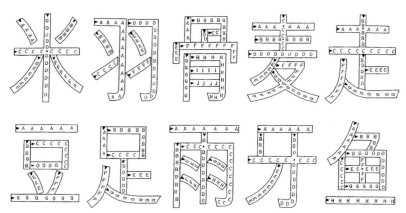

Proverb Wisdom

【如ke 鱼sh 得t 水er】 (like · fish · get · water)

☞ *like a fish that got water*

Explanation : feel just like fish in water

Example   : He got some friends to help him in the work, and he felt ***like a fish in water*** (→ *like a fish that got water*).

Hanzi Combinations

【羽化】 (feather・concert) .... enclosion, become an immortal
【羽族】 (feather・clan) .... birds
【骨肉】 (bone・flesh) .... kindred (feelings)
【骨气】 (bone・spirit) .... moral integrity
【走红】 (walk・red) .... be in luck
【鱼雷】 (fish・thunder) .... torpedo

Street Hanzi

★ 柯达快速冲印 ＝ Kodak speedy develop & print
★ 2小时取 ＝ You can take in 2 hours

stalk・reach	fast・speed	flush・print	2 little・time	take
柯达	快速	冲印	2 小时	取
Kodak	speedy	develop & print	in 2 hours	take

47

Reading Hanzi

More Intelligent in Dreams

When a student failed to solve a math problem in class, 他e expressed 他s regret to 他s teacher.

"我 记er solving the problem in 我y 梦m last 夜t, 但t for the 时me being 我've forgotten it. What 能n that mean?"

"It means that 你u are 更re intelligent in 梦ms than when 你u are awake," the teacher explained.

New Hanzi

他e	he	夜t	night
他s	his	但t	but
我	I	时me	time
我y	my	能n	can
记er	remember	你u	you
梦m	dream	更re	more

Reading Hanzi-Practice

① 他e is 二o years 老der than 我.
② Do 你u know 他s phone number?
③ 我 am not wrong.
④ It's 我e.
⑤ 我e, too.
⑥ Not that 我 记er.
⑦ Now 我 记er
⑧ live in a 梦m
⑨ Sweet 梦ms!
⑩ last 夜t

⑪ Good 夜t!
⑫ No 但ts!
⑬ We could 见ee nothing 但t 水er.
⑭ all the 时me
⑮ from 时me to 时me
⑯ I 能n 但t do 我y best.
⑰ 能n 我 help 你u?
⑱ How are 你u?
⑲ much 更re
⑳ no 更re

English Reading

① He is two years older than I. ② Do you know his phone number?
③ I am not wrong. ④ It's me. ⑤ Me, too. ⑥ Not that I remember.
⑦ Now I remember ⑧ live in a dream ⑨ Sweet dreams! ⑩ last night
⑪ Good night! ⑫ No buts! ⑬ We could see nothing but water.
⑭ all the time ⑮ from time to time ⑯ I can but do my best.
⑰ Can I help you? ⑱ How are you? ⑲ much more ⑳ no more

Hanzi Colum

鱼 (fish)

This is a typical hieroglyphic Chinese character. At first the character 鱼 (fish) was formed with all its external parts such as head, eyeball, body, scales, fin and tail etc. Later, it was simplified and the components were limited to the head, body and tail. Its tail was something like the character 火 (fire). Later it became four slashes, and eventually became simply a horizontal line.

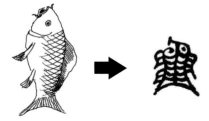

Writing Hanzi

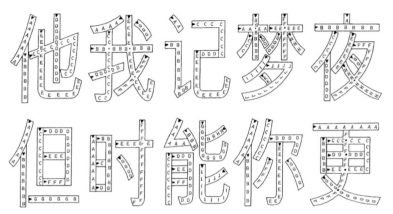

Proverb Wisdom

【不t 失se 时me 机ce】(not・lose・time・chance)

☞ *not to lose the time and chance*

Explanation : not to lose the chance / lose no time

Example : The important thing in business is ***not to lose a good chance***

(→ *not to lose the time and chance*).

【我 行t 我y 素t】(I・act・my・element)

☞ *I act as I usually act*

Explanation : persist in one's old ways no matter what others say / the dogs bark, but the caravan goes on

Example : ***He persists in his old ways*** (→ *He acts as he usually acts*) no matter what others say.

Hanzi Combinations

【他们】(he · plural) .... they
【记者】(record · er) .... journalist
【梦话】(dream · words) .... somniloquy
【夜光】(night · light) .... luminous
【夜曲】(night · melody) .... nocturne
【时装】(time · dress) .... fashion

Street Hanzi

★ 登机口 = boarding gate

ascend · machine (plane)　　　mouth
　　登机　　　　　　　　　　　口
　　boarding　　　　　　　　　gate

Reading Hanzi

The Same Language

A girl who 要ted to terminate her friendship with her 男y 友d 说d to him:

"Sorry, we don't seem to 有ve anything in 共n to continue our friendship."

"But we do have one thing in common. We 说k the 同me 语ge, don't we?" the boy 应ied with a 惑led look.

New Hanzi

要t	want	有ve	have	语ge	language
男y	boy	共n	common	应y	reply
友d	friend	说k	speak	惑le	puzzle
说d	said	同me	same		

Reading Hanzi–Practice

① 要t for nothing
② 要t ad
③ college 男y
④ 男y scout
⑤ pen 友d
⑥ One of my 友ds 说d.
⑦ 说d person
⑧ 我 有ve a brother.
⑨ 我 don't 有ve any cash with 我e.
⑩ 共n sense
⑪ 共n law
⑫ strictly 说king
⑬ 说k out
⑭ just the 同me
⑮ 同me to 你u
⑯ 说ken 语ge
⑰ written 语ge
⑱ What did 你u 说y in 应y?
⑲ 应y card
⑳ a 惑le ring
㉑ a crossword 惑le

English Reading

① want for nothing ② want ad ③ college boy ④ boy scout ⑤ pen friend
⑥ One of my friends said. ⑦ said person ⑧ I have a brother.
⑨ I don't have any cash with me. ⑩ common sense ⑪ common law
⑫ strictly speaking ⑬ speak out ⑭ just the same ⑮ same to you
⑯ spoken language ⑰ written language ⑱ What did you say in reply?
⑲ reply card ⑳ a puzzle ring ㉑ a crossword puzzle

Hanzi Colum

有 (have)

The original meaning of the character 有 (have) was acquisition. I.e., grasping something by hand and possessing it. In the Jiaguwen era the hand (手) was usually depicted as 又 , and 又 was used as 有 (have) for a long time. During the Jinwen era, under the 又 , the character 月 (simplified from 肉 meaning meat) was added, - meaning that a man grasped the meat with his hand. Thus the present Chinese character 有 (have) was formed.

Writing Hanzi

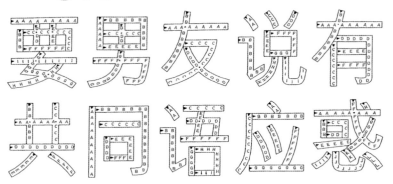

Proverb Wisdom

【岂w 有ve 此s 理le】 (how · have · this · rule)

☞ *How do you have this kind of rule?*

Explanation : there is no such rule

Example　: You put forward such a silly proposal to your boss. ***This is really outrageous*** (→*How do you have this kind of rule*).

【同me 舟t 共er 济s】 (same · boat · together · cross)

☞ *to cross together in the same boat*

Explanation : cross a river in the same boat

Example　: We must ***stand together in all weathers*** (→*cross together in the same boat*) in the fight against corruption.

Hanzi Combinations

【说亲】 (speak · intimate) .... matchmake
【有机】 (have · mechanism) .... organic
【有钱】 (have · monney) .... rich; wealthy
【有喜】 (have · happy) .... pregnant
【共产】 (common · wealth) .... communism
【共和】 (common · peace) .... republicanism

Street Hanzi

★ 中国电信 ＝ China Telecom
★ 公用电话 ＝ public telephone

central · country	electric · letter	public · use	electric · speak
中国	电信	公用	电话
China	Telecom	public	telephone

Reading **H**anzi

I'm Afraid of That, Too

后r 些me laborious 时rs at 她r painting, 她e rose 和d called her 夫d, a countryside painter.

"来me and look at my 画re, dear. I'm so satisfied with the result that I'm afraid people will mistake it for your work."

"I'm 恐d of 那t, 也o," the husband replied, after careful study of the painting.

New Hanzi

后r	after	和d	and	那t	that
些me	some	夫d	husband	也o	too
时r	hour	来me	come		
她r	her	画re	picture		
她e	she	恐d	afraid		

Reading Hanzi–Practice

① 些me other 时me
② 些me money
③ keep early 时rs
④ 时r hand
⑤ 她r hair falls past 她r shoulder.
⑥ 她e is Mrs. Black.
⑦ a 她e-goat
⑧ fruit 和d cream
⑨ 和d so forth
⑩ He was a good 夫d to her.
⑪ 来me what may
⑫ 来me forth
⑬ pretty as a 画re
⑭ 画re window
⑮ Don't be 恐d, dear.
⑯ He was 恐d of losing face.
⑰ 那t is it.
⑱ 那t's 那t.
⑲ 我e, 也o.
⑳ 我 had a stomachache 和 d a headache, 也o.

English Reading

① some other time ② some money ③ keep early hours ④ hour hand
⑤ Her hair falls past her shoulder. ⑥ She is Mrs. Black. ⑦ a she-goat
⑧ fruit and cream ⑨ and so forth ⑩ He was a good husband to her.
⑪ come what may ⑫ come forth ⑬ pretty as a picture ⑭ picture window
⑮ Don't be afraid, dear. ⑯ He was afraid of losing face. ⑰ That is it.
⑱ That's that. ⑲ Me, too. ⑳ I had a stomachache and a headache, too.

Hanzi Colum

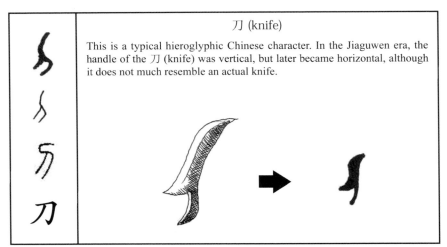

刀 (knife)

This is a typical hieroglyphic Chinese character. In the Jiaguwen era, the handle of the 刀 (knife) was vertical, but later became horizontal, although it does not much resemble an actual knife.

Writing **H**anzi

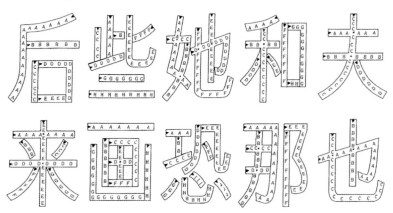

Proverb Wisdom

【心t 口th 如s 一ne】 (heart · mouth · as · one)

☞ *one's heart and mouth same as one*

Explanation : say what one thinks

Example : I don't think *he has come out with what's really on his mind* (→ his heart and mouth same as one).

【时me 不t 我s 待t】 (time · not · us · wait)

☞ *time does not wait for us*

Explanation : time and waves wait for no man

Example : *Time and waves wait for no man* (→ *Time does not wait for us*). We must make good use of our time.

Hanzi Combinations

【夫人】 (husband's • person) .... wife
【画皮】 (paint • skin) .... mask (one's disguise)
【恐怖】 (horror • fear) .... terror
【恐龙】 (horror • dragon) .... dinosaur
【也许】 (also • promise) .... maybe

Street Hanzi

★ 出租车 候客站 = Taxi's waiting stop

outer • lease • car	wait • guest	station
出租车	候客	站
Taxi's	waiting	stop

Reading Hanzi

Someday They Will Be on Fire

Alice was so 厌ted at her husband's 烟te smoking that she 诉ned to him one day.

"I 盼pe that all the cigarette factories 将l 抓ch fire someday."

"勿t worry, dear. 全l the cigarettes will be 设t on fire," he said with a 莞le.

New Hanzi

厌t	disgust	将l	will	设t	set
烟te	cigarette	抓ch	catch	莞le	smile
诉n	complain	勿t	don't		
盼pe	hope	全l	all		

Reading Hanzi–Practice

① The smell of 鱼sh 厌ts 我e.
② 我 感lt 厌t 在t 他s bad behavior.
③ 烟te holder
④ light 一 烟te
⑤ 诉n of 一 牙thache
⑥ 你u 有ve nothing to 诉n about, 干o 你u?
⑦ 盼pe chest
⑧ 盼pe against 盼pe
⑨ 那t 将l 干o.
⑩ Boys 将l be boys.
⑪ 抓ch phrase
⑫ play 抓ch
⑬ 勿t forget!
⑭ 勿t touch it!
⑮ 全l right
⑯ 不t 在t 全l.
⑰ 设t out
⑱ 请se 设t these 皿shes on the table.
⑲ The weather 莞led on them.
⑳ with 一 莞le

English Reading

① The smell of fish disgusts me. ② I felt disgust at his bad behavior.
③ cigarette holder ④ light a cigarette ⑤ complain of a toothache
⑥ You have nothing to complain about, do you? ⑦ hope chest
⑧ hope against hope ⑨ That will do. ⑩ Boys will be boys.
⑪ catch phrase ⑫ play catch ⑬ Don't forget! ⑭ Don't touch it!
⑮ all right ⑯ Not at all. ⑰ set out ⑱ Please set these dishes on the table.
⑲ The weather smiled on them. ⑳ with a smile

Hanzi Colum

小 (small)

During the Jiaguwen and Jinwen eras, the character 小 (small) was depicted with three short vertical lines representing three grains of sand. Later, the three vertical lines became longer, and the lines on the left and right became tilted, forming the present character 小 (small).

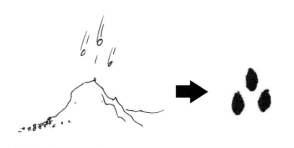

Writing Hanzi

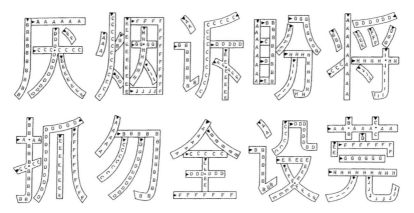

Proverb Wisdom

【兵er 不t 厌te 诈t】 (soldier · not · hate · cheat)

☞ ***Soldiers don't hate the cheat.***

Explanation : All is fair in war.

Example : There is an old saying: ***All is fair in war*** (→ *The soldiers don't hate the cheat*). So we can pretend to be defeated.

【将ng 计ck 就1 计ck】 (bring · trick · deal · trick)

☞ ***to bring out a trick to deal with one's trick***

Explanation : turn someone's trick against him

Example : Tom pretended to be ill and the manager ***beat him at his own game*** (→ *bring out a trick to deal with his trick*) and fired him.

Hanzi Combinations

【厌世】 (disgust · world) .... pessimistic
【厌食】 (disgust · food) .... anorexia
【眼波】 (eye · wave) .... glances (of a young lady)
【眼色】 (eye · color) .... a hint given with glance
【设备】 (set · prepare)................................... equipment

Street Hanzi

★ 售票处 = Ticket Office

sell · ticket · place
售 票 处
Ticket Office

UNIT 15

Reading Hanzi

I am Not Listening

于n 班s a girl student was 瞧king at a small 镜r while 梳mbing her 发r and doing her make-up. The 师er noticed and 评ted.

"You shouldn't do your make-up while 听ning to class."

And the student said, "That's 行K. I am not listening while doing my make-up."

Reading Hanzi–Practice

① 于n the yard
② 于n that
③ the 班s of 1999
④ a French 班s
⑤ have a 瞧k
⑥ at the first 瞧k
⑦ a rearview 镜r
⑧ 镜r image
⑨ 你u need a good 梳mb.
⑩ 梳mb out

⑪ split 发rs
⑫ 发ir oil
⑬ a music 师er
⑭ Our 师er is strict.
⑮ No 评t.
⑯ Do 你u 有ve any 评ts?
⑰ 听n to the music
⑱ 勿t 听n to 她r.
⑲ It's 行K with 我e.
⑳ Everything 将l go 行K.

English Reading

① in the yard ② in that ③ the class of 1999 ④ a French class
⑤ have a look ⑥ at the first look ⑦ a rearview mirror ⑧ mirror image
⑨ You need a good comb. ⑩ comb out ⑪ split hairs ⑫ hair oil
⑬ a music teacher ⑭ Our teacher is strict. ⑮ No comment.
⑯ Do you have any comments? ⑰ listen to the music ⑱ Don't listen to her.
⑲ It's OK with me. ⑳ Everything will go OK.

Hanzi Colum

大 (large)

The Chinese character 大 represents a person who spread his arms to explain the size of something. One opinion says that man of primitive ages thought themselves great and used the character 人 (person) with his feet spread wide, standing on the ground to depict the meaning of large.

Writing Hanzi

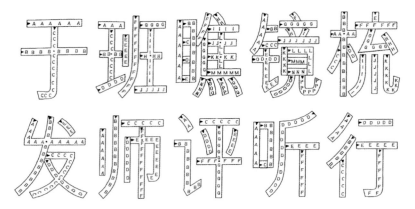

Proverb Wisdom

【洗sh 耳rs 恭ly 听n】 (wash · ears · respectfully · listen)

☞ *to wash one's ears and listen respectfully*

Explanation : listen with respectful attention

Example   : He *lent an attentive ear* (→ *washed his ears and listened respectfully*) to the words of wisdom .

【听n 天n 由w 命y】 (listen · heaven · follow · destiny)

☞ *listen to heaven and follow one's destiny*

Explanation : trust to luck

Example   : Once you've sown, you just have to *trust to luck* (→ *listen to heaven and follow your destiny*).

Hanzi Combinations

【班房】(class・house) .... jail
【发菜】(hair・vegetable) .... flagelliform nostoc
【发蜡】(hair・wax) .... pomade
【听从】(listen・follow) .... obey
【听写】(listen・write) .... dictation

Street Hanzi

★ 北二出口 = the No.2 North Exit

north	two	out・mouth
北	二	出口
north	No.2	Exit

Reading Hanzi

Like Mother, Like Daughter

My husband, a 高gh 校l teacher, had a 会ting with the mother 于f a student who had a tendency to 成me distracted during class. He 问ked her if she had noticed that problem 当n dealing with her daughter. The mother looked thoughtfully at him and then 点ted to the 远r 墙l. "Are those aluminum 窗ws?" She asked.

New Hanzi

高gh	high	成me	become	远r	far
校l	school	问k	ask	墙l	wall
会t	meet	当n	when	窗w	window
于f	of	点t	point		

Reading Hanzi–Practice

① fly 高gh
② 我 searched 高gh and low.
③ 后r 校l
④ cut 校l
⑤ a track 会t
⑥ Does this 会t 你r wishes?
⑦ What has 成me of him?
⑧ 她e 成ame a lawyer.
⑨ the driver 于f the car
⑩ a cup 于f coffee
⑪ 他e 问ked 后r 你u.
⑫ May 我 问k a question?
⑬ 当n 我 was a 儿d
⑭ 当n 于n trouble, visit this man.
⑮ 点t the way
⑯ the boiling 点t
⑰ a 远r cry
⑱ So 远r so good.
⑲ drive a person to the 墙l
⑳ go to the 墙l

English Reading

① fly high ② I searched high and low. ③ after school ④ cut school
⑤ a track meet ⑥ Does this meet your wishes? ⑦ What has become of him?
⑧ She became a lawyer. ⑨ the diver of the car ⑩ a cup of coffee
⑪ He asked after you. ⑫ May I ask a question? ⑬ when I was a child
⑭ When in trouble, visit this man. ⑮ point the way ⑯ the boiling point
⑰ a far cry ⑱ So far so good. ⑲ drive a person to the wall ⑳ go to the wall

Hanzi Colum

高 (high)

The Chinese character 高 (high) shows an ancient Chinese high building. The upper part of the character shows the sharp roof of a building but has now become ⼇. However the remaining lower part has retained the shape of a building.

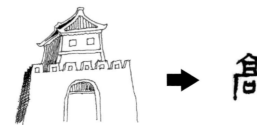

Writing Hanzi

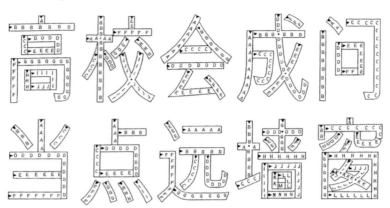

Proverb Wisdom

【敬t 而d 远r 之t】 (respect · and · far · it)

☞ *to respect and be far from someone*

Explanation : stand aloof from someone courteously / the best defense against a bad man is to keep far away

Example : The secretary ***keeps a respectful distance from*** (→ *respects and be far from*) her boss .

【不t 耻me 下d 问k】 (not · shame · descend · ask)

☞ *don't be ashamed to descend to ask*

Explanation : not feel shamed to ask one's subordinate

Example : The learned are ***not above asking questions and learning from the less educated*** (→ *not be ashamed to descend to ask*).

Hanzi Combinations

【高明】(high · bright) .... wise; clever
【高原】(high · champaign) .... plateau
【远古】(far · old) .... remote antiquity
【远足】(far · foot) .... hike
【问题】(ask · title) .... problem

Street Hanzi

★ 香港名店街 = Hong Kong Famous Shops Street

fragrant · harbor   famous · shop · street
香港   **名店街**
Hong Kong   Famous Shops Street

71

UNIT 17

Reading Hanzi

Prayer in the School

Since President Clinton 呼led for 静t 祷yer in 公c schools, it has become a 烦xing public issue. 请se imagine the picture of a typical pupil in prayer.

Pupil A: Oh, God, let the 铃l ring now ⋯

Pupil B: 主d, make these pimples go away ⋯

Pupil C: Dear 神d, make Dianna like me ⋯

Pupil D: Please, God, let our teacher be 病l tomorrow ⋯

New Hanzi

呼l	call	烦x	vex	神d	God
静t	silent	请se	please	病l	ill
祷y	pray	铃l	bell		
公c	public	主d	lord		

Reading Hanzi–Practice

① 呼l back
② 呼l a strike
③ a 静t volcano
④ a 静t letter
⑤ He 祷yed for 神d's forgiveness.
⑥ 祷ying mantis
⑦ the 公c good
⑧ a 公c library
⑨ 我 was 烦xed with him.
⑩ 来me 于n, 请se.
⑪ This way, 请se.
⑫ That name rings a 铃l.
⑬ answer the 铃l
⑭ the 主d's Supper
⑮ live like a 主d
⑯ by 神d
⑰ Money is 他s 神d.
⑱ She is very 病l with a fever.

English Reading

① call back ② call a strike ③ a silent volcano ④ a silent letter
⑤ He prayed for God's forgiveness. ⑥ praying mantis ⑦ the public good
⑧ a public library ⑨ I was vexed with him. ⑩ Come in, please.
⑪ This way, please. ⑫ That name rings a bell. ⑬ answer the bell
⑭ the Lord's Supper ⑮ live like a lord ⑯ by God ⑰ Money is his God.
⑱ She is very ill with a fever.

Hanzi Colum

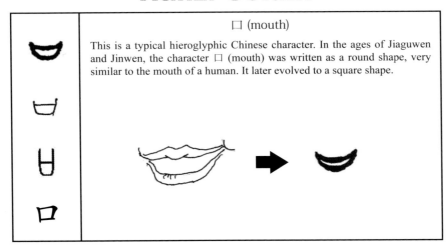

口 (mouth)

This is a typical hieroglyphic Chinese character. In the ages of Jiaguwen and Jinwen, the character 口 (mouth) was written as a round shape, very similar to the mouth of a human. It later evolved to a square shape.

Writing Hanzi

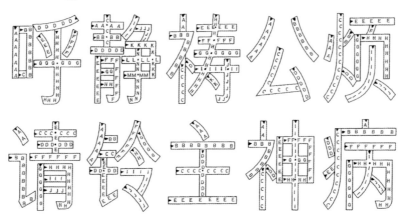

Proverb Wisdom

【先st 入er 为e 主n】 (first · enter · be · main)

☞ *what entered first be main*

Explanation : first impressions are strongest

Example : ***First impressions are the strongest*** (→ *What entered first be main*).
So you should make a good impression right away.

【齐n 心ts 协t 力ers】 (even · hearts · joint · powers)

☞ *even up one's hearts and joint one's powers*

Explanation : pull all together

Example : Let's ***pull together*** (→ *even up our hearts and joint our powers*)
and finish the work as soon as possible.

Hanzi Combinations

【公害】 (public · harassment) .... enviroment pollution
【公司】 (public · manage) .... company
【主妇】 (master · woman) .... housewife
【主席】 (master · seat) .... chairman
【呼吸】 (exhale · inhale) .... breathe

Street Hanzi

★ 新北京 新奥运 = New Beijing; New Olympic Games

new	north · capital		new	Olympic · motion
新	北京		新	奥运
New	Beijing		New	Olympic Games

Reading **H**anzi

Spanish Effect

I 教t an adult 英sh-as-a-second-language class that consisted of all Spanish-speaking students 除t one. He was a young man 从m India whom we called Mike. After several months of night school, one of the students, who 待yed after class, 述ked, "When Mike first came to class, he couldn't speak any English." She 顿sed, and 聿n 加ded, "现w, he can speak Spanish."

New Hanzi

教t	taught	待y	stay	加d	add
英sh	English	述k	remark	现w	now
除t	except	顿se	pause		
从m	from	聿n	then		

Reading Hanzi–Practice

① 我y 父er 教t us swimming.
② 教ch 校l
③ 英sh breakfast
④ 英sh Channel
⑤ They 除t John 从m the list.
⑥ present company 除ted
⑦ 从m 现w on
⑧ 从m beginning to end
⑨ The guest 述ked ironically.
⑩ 勿t make rude 述ks.

⑪ 待y put
⑫ 来me to 待y
⑬ make a 顿se
⑭ give a person 顿se
⑮ 现w and 聿n
⑯ there and 聿n
⑰ up to 现w
⑱ 加d up to
⑲ 将l 你u 加d 更re sugar?

English Reading

① My father taught us swimming. ② teach school ③ English breakfast
④ English Channel ⑤ They except John from the list.
⑥ present company excepted ⑦ from now on ⑧ from beginning to end
⑨ The guest remarked ironically. ⑩ Don't make rude remarks. ⑪ stay put
⑫ come to stay ⑬ make a pause ⑭ give a person pause ⑮ now and then
⑯ there and then ⑰ up to now ⑱ add up to ⑲ Will you add more sugar?

Hanzi Colum

从 (follow)

From the time of the Jiaguwen, the Chinese character 从 (follow) represented a condition where a person (人) follows close behind another person (人). For a long time, the Chinese character 从 (follow) was also written as 從 , but since 1950, it was returned to the Jiaguwen symbol 从 . Now the character 从 has another main meaning: from.

Writing Hanzi

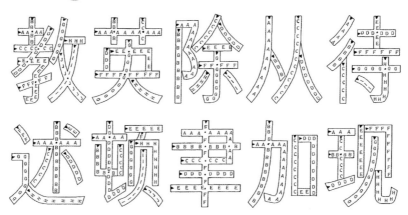

Proverb Wisdom

【大t 器l 晚te 成te】 (great · vessel · late · complete)

☞ *a great vessel will be completed late*

Explanation : a great man will take time to shape and mature

Example   : His success in painting at the age of forty showed that ***his talent had matured slowly*** (→ *a great vessel will be completed late*).

【刀d 山ns 火re 海as】 (sword · mountains · fire · seas)

☞ *sword mountains and fire seas*

Explanation : a mountain of swords and a sea of flame / most severe trial

Example   : In order to protect the country from attack, the soldiers will never retreat before ***an extremely dangerous place*** (→ *sword mountains and fire seas*).

Hanzi Combinations

【教练】(teach・excersise) .... coach
【教育】(teach・bring-up) .... education
【加班】(add・shift) .... work overtime
【加油】(add・oil) .... Come on! Come on! (make an extra effort)
【英语】(English・language)) .... English

Street Hanzi

★ 梦园珠宝 = Dream-Round Jewelry

dream・round   pearl・treasure
梦园   珠宝
Dream-Round   Jewelry

UNIT 19

Reading Hanzi

Busy with Appointments

Two friends meet in the 街t and the following conversation 取kes 处ce:

Jane : I haven't seen you recently. 何t are you 忙y 在t?

Mary : Well, you 知w, I have so 多y appointments with my doctor these days.

Jane : What's wrong with you?

Mary : 无ng 误ng with me physically. The doctor is my fiancé.

Reading Hanzi–Practice

① 走k the 街ts
② 街t kid
③ 取ke it or leave it
④ 取ke out
⑤ 处ce card
⑥ put a person 于n 他s 处ce
⑦ Do 何t it 取kes.
⑧ So 何t!
⑨ a 忙y day
⑩ The line is 忙y.

⑪ 二o nations 在t war
⑫ 在t that
⑬ You never 知w.
⑭ 知w-how
⑮ so 多y
⑯ a great 多y
⑰ 来me to 无ng
⑱ for 无ng
⑲ get it 误ng
⑳ a 误ng answer

English Reading

① walk the streets ② street kid ③ take it or leave it ④ take out
⑤ place card ⑥ put a person in his place ⑦ Do what it takes. ⑧ So what!
⑨ a busy day ⑩ The line is busy. ⑪ two nations at war ⑫ at that
⑬ You never know. ⑭ know-how ⑮ so many ⑯ a great many
⑰ come to nothing ⑱ for nothing ⑲ get it wrong ⑳ a wrong answer

Hanzi Colum

巾 (towel)

This character's original meaning was towel or dishcloth. Normally a towel was always hung to dry on a cruciform (十) type of hanger, so the symbol became 巾 .

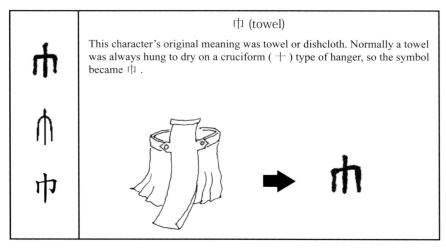

Writing Hanzi

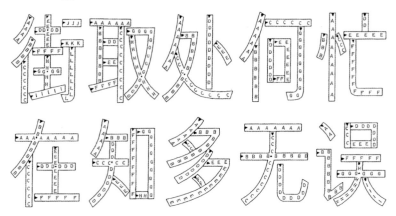

Proverb Wisdom

【断t 章er 取ke 义ng】 (cut · chapter · take · meaning)

☞ *to cut words from whole chapter and take the meaning*

Explanation : make a deliberate misinterpretation out of context

Example : The author was upset because some readers *distorted the meaning* (→ *cut words from whole chapter and take the meaning*) in his novel.

【迫ch 在t 眉w 睫sh】 (approach · at · brow · eyelash)

☞ *to approach the brows and eyelashes*

Explanation : of the utmost urgency

Example : To save the child's life is a matter *of great urgency* (→ *which approaches the brows and eyelashes*)for the doctor.

Hanzi Combinations

【取缔】 (take · conclude) .... ban, suppress
【处死】 (place · dead) .... execute
【何不】 (what · not) .... why not
【知心】 (know · heart) .... intimate
【在野党】 (at · field · party) .... a party not in office

Street Hanzi

★ 无痛穿耳 ＝ No pain earlobe pierce

no · pain   pierce · ear

无痛   穿耳
No pain   earlobe pierce

UNIT 20

Reading Hanzi

Me Only a Fool

Robert works in the telegram 段n of a city 邮t 署ce. He's used to 读ding various 略ns and usually has no trouble understanding any of them. One day, however, he was puzzled by a cryptic telegram handed 过r by a young student. It read: "Me, 仅y a fool."

Robert could not help asking the student. The student explained that he had written a 信r to his father asking him for a camera. His father 占ned two cameras, one of which bore the 牌d "Fool".

New Hanzi

段n	section	略n	omission	占n	own
邮t	post	过r	over	牌d	brand
署ce	office	仅y	only		
读d	read	信r	letter		

Reading Hanzi–Practice

① Japanese 段n
② 段n mark
③ keep a person 邮ted
④ He 邮ted the book to 我e.
⑤ 读d between the lines
⑥ 请se 读d "他e" as "她e."
⑦ correct the 略n
⑧ 我y 占n idea
⑨ They 工k 于n their 占n cars.
⑩ Who 占ns this land?

⑪ 过r and 过r 又n
⑫ 时me is 过r.
⑬ an open 信r
⑭ a 信r 于f introduction
⑮ 我y 仅y 女l
⑯ 仅y two
⑰ They 牌ded him a traitor.
⑱ 牌d-new
⑲ the Foreign 署ce
⑳ Head 署ce

English Reading

① Japanese section ② section mark ③ keep a person posted
④ He posted the book to me. ⑤ read between the lines
⑥ Please read "he" as "she." ⑦ correct the omission ⑧ my own idea
⑨ They work in their own cars. ⑩ Who owns this land? ⑪ over and over again
⑫ Time is over. ⑬ an open letter ⑭ a letter of introduction ⑮ my only girl
⑯ only two ⑰ They branded him a traitor. ⑱ brand-new
⑲ the Foreign Office ⑳ Head Office

Hanzi Colum

工 (work)

The character 工 (work) dates back to the early Jinwen era. The form of the character shows the shape of a stock ax. The lower part of the blade was a circular arc shape, but later it became 口 . Finally it became only a horizontal line, the same as the top part of the character. The original meaning of the Chinese character 工 (work) was tool.

Writing **H**anzi

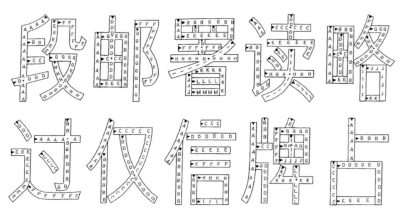

Proverb Wisdom

【力th 不t 从w 心t】 (strength · not · follow · heart)

☞ *one's strength can't follow his heart*

Explanation : one's ambition far exceeds one's power

Example : I an willing to help you, but *it is beyond my power* (→ *my strength can't follow my heart*).

【日ly 理le 万d 机rs】 (daily · handle · ten-thousand · affairs)

☞ *to handle ten-thousand affairs daily*

Explanation : be busy with myriad of affairs

Example : He *busied himself with many affairs every day* (→ *handled ten-thousand affairs daily*) but never stopping his study.

Hanzi Combinations

【过敏】(over · nimble) .... allergy
【过时】(over · time) .... outdate
【信鸽】(letter · pigeon) .... carrier, pigeon

Street Hanzi

★ 上海明君书店 ＝ Shanghai Brilliant-King Book Store

upper · sea	brilliant · king	book · shop
上海	明君	书店
Shanghai	Brilliant-King	Book Store

Reading Hanzi

Even Better?

(A) The 别er day I met my Chinese friend Mr. Deng. He had been 学ying English at night school for 约t two 年rs.

"How are you getting 在n with your English, Deng?" I asked him.

"Oh, 颇te 好l. Sometimes I 感l my English is 佳er 过n my Chinese." He articulated with pride.

"真ly?" I could not hold 返k my disbelief. "How do you know?"

"Well, often when I speak English, I don't know its Chinese meaning."

(B) The 别er day 我 met 我y Chinese 友d Mr. Deng. 他e had been 学ying 英sh at 夜t 校l for 约t 二o 年rs.

"How are 你u getting on with your 英sh, Deng?" 我 问ked him.

"Oh, 颇te 好l. Sometimes 我 感l 我y 英sh is 佳er 过n 我y Chinese." 他e articulated with pride.

"真ly?" 我 could not hold 返k 我y disbelief. "How do 你u 知w?"

"好l, often 当n 我 说k 英sh, 我 don't 知w its Chinese meaning."

New Hanzi

别er	other	在n	on	佳er	better
学y	study	颇te	quite	过n	than
约t	about	好l	well	真ly	really
年r	year	感l	feel	返k	back

Reading Hanzi–Practice

① the 别er world
② among 别ers
③ 于n a brown 学y
④ Chinese 学ies
⑤ 他e is 约t 你r age.
⑥ 我 met him 约t noon.
⑦ 从m 年r to 年r
⑧ 全l 年r round
⑨ be 颇te the thing
⑩ 颇te a few
⑪ 好l and truly

⑫ 好l 现w!
⑬ 感l good
⑭ 感l 好l
⑮ for 佳er, for worse
⑯ so much the 佳er
⑰ none 别er 过n
⑱ 我 知w 你u 佳er 过n 她e.
⑲ a 真ly funny show
⑳ 我 don't 真ly like potatoes.
㉑ 瞧k 返k
㉒ 我 hit him 返k.

English Reading

① the other world ② among others ③ in a brown study ④ Chinese studies
⑤ He is about your age. ⑥ I met him about noon. ⑦ from year to year
⑧ all year round ⑨ be quite the thing ⑩ quite a few ⑪ well and truly
⑫ Well now! ⑬ feel good ⑭ feel well ⑮ for better, for worse ⑯ so much the better
⑰ none other than ⑱ I know you better than she. ⑲ a really funny show
⑳ I don't really like potatoes. ㉑ look back ㉒ I hit him back.

Hanzi Colum

王 (king)

Originally the character 王 (king) was a picture of a large ax. The top part was its handle, the middle part was the shaft, and the lower part was the arc-shaped axe blade. Later, the lower part became a horizontal line, and eventually became the present character 王 (king). In ancient China, the ultimate ruler of a country had the right to decide the life or death of any citizen, and the ax symbolized this right.

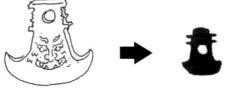

Writing Hanzi

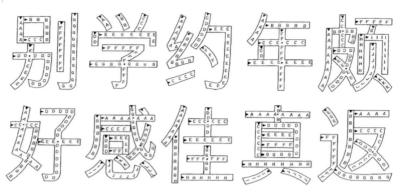

Proverb Wisdom

【百d 年rs 大ge 计me】 (hundred · years · large · scheme)

☞ *a large scheme for hundred years*

Explanation : a hundred years plan

Example   : The construction of a new way from North to South is ***a project of vital and lasting importance*** (→ *a large stratagem for hundred years*).

【守d 口th 如ke 瓶le】 (guard · mouth · like · bottle)

☞ *to guard one's mouth like a bottle with a plug*

Explanation : keep one's mouth closed

Example   : He was ordered to ***make an absolute secrecy of*** (→ *guard his mouth like a bottle with a plug*) concerning this matter.

Hanzi Combinations

【学分制】 (study · point · system) .... the credit system
【学究】 (study · research) .... pedant
【学友】 (study · friend) .... schoolmate
【年谱】 (year · tables) .... chronological life
【感恩节】 (feel · kindness · festival) .... Thanksgiving Day

Street Hanzi

★ 中国烟草 = China Tobacco

central · country   smoke · grass
中国   烟草
China   Tobacco

UNIT 22

Reading Hanzi

Pay Special Attention to the Way the Chinese Speak English

(A) An American student studying in China 觉d it 难t to speak idiomatic 汉se. One day he asked his room-伙te who was also 学ning Chinese. "Sometimes I have the same problem. But from my personal experience, I have 意ced that you would 健d more Chinese the 道y the Chinese speak English. For 例le, 'I 翌t year will from Beijing language 院te graduate.'"

(B) An American student 学ying 于n China 觉d it 难t to 说k idiomatic 汉se. 一ne day 他e 问ked 他s room-伙te who was 也o 学ning 汉se. "Sometimes 我 有ve the 同me problem. 但t 从m 我y personal experience, 我 have 意ced 那t 你u would 健d 更re 汉se the 道y the 汉se 说k 英sh. For 例le, '我 翌t 年r 将l 从m Beijing 语ge 院te graduate.'"

New Hanzi

觉d	found	学n	learn	例le	example
难t	difficult	意ce	notice	翌t	next
汉se	Chinese	健d	sound	院te	institute
伙te	mate	道y	way		

Reading Hanzi–Practice

① I 觉d the book very interesting.
② 我 呼led 在n 她r 和d 觉d that 她e was out.
③ 难t task
④ 难t 儿d
⑤ 汉se character
⑥ 汉se lantern
⑦ We are 伙tes.
⑧ the 伙te to this shoe
⑨ 在n short 意ce
⑩ 意ce board
⑪ A 健d mind 于n a 健d body.
⑫ This bridge is still 健d.
⑬ No 道y!
⑭ put a person out 于f the 道y
⑮ as an 例le
⑯ for 例le
⑰ 于n the 翌t 处ce
⑱ 翌t to none
⑲ The 英sh 语ge 院te
⑳ Massachusetts 院te 于f Technology
㉑ 学ned the poem by 心t
㉒ 人le 学n 从m experience.

English Reading

① I found the book very interesting. ② I called on her and found that she was out.
③ difficult task ④ difficult child ⑤ Chinese character ⑥ Chinese lantern
⑦ We are mates. ⑧ the mate to this shoe ⑨ on short notice ⑩ notice board
⑪ A sound mind in a sound body. ⑫ This bridge is still sound. ⑬ No way!
⑭ put a person out of the way ⑮ as an example ⑯ for example
⑰ in the next place ⑱ next to none ⑲ The English Language Institute
⑳ Massachusetts Institute of Technology ㉑ learned the poem by heart
㉒ People learn from experience.

Hanzi Colum

门 (door)

Anyone who has seen a Chinese gate will recognize this hieroglyph. In the Jiaguwen and Jinwen eras normally two gates were depicted. At the first stage there was also a crossbar on the top, making it look just like an actual door. The character 門 (door) was later simplified to 门 .

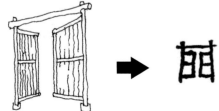

Writing **H**anzi

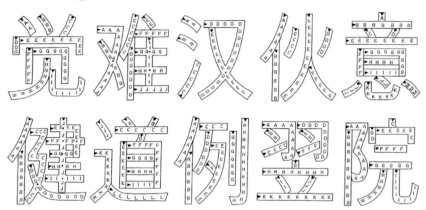

Proverb Wisdom

【本t 性er 难t 移ve】 (root · character · difficult · move)

> ☞ *It is difficult to move the root of the character.*

Explanation : be difficult to alter one's character

Example : I advised him to give up smoking, but he won't. It is too *difficult to change his character*. (→ *difficult to move the root of the character*).

【千d 载rs 难t 逢t】 (thousand · years · difficult · meet)

> ☞ *it is difficult to meet even in thousand years*

Explanation : a very rare oppotunity

Example : This chance *comes once in a blue moon* (→ *is difficult to meet even in thousand years*).

Hanzi Combinations

【学分制】 (learn · point · system) .... the credit system
【学舌】 (learn · tongue) .... parrot; ape
【难色】 (difficult · color) .... a reluctant or embarrassed expression
【难看】 (difficult · see) .... ugly
【例外】 (exmple · out) .... exception

Street Hanzi

复旦大学正门

★ 复旦大学正门 = the main gate of Fudan University (A famous
university in China)

again · dawn	large · study	straight · door
复旦	大学	正门
Fudan	University	gate

UNIT 23

Reading Hanzi

The Plane Crashed

(A) Authony Nesty is a black athlete from Suriname. He was the world champion in the men's 100 meters' 蝶y 泳mming. But in the Barcelona Olympic 娱mes he 获red only a bronze medal. When a 报ter interviewed him, he said,

"During the 赛ch, the spectators all 叫ted 欢y and encouragement to me: 'Mr. Plane, 励r up!' But unfortunately, the plane 坠shed tonight."

(B) Authony Nesty is a black athlete 从m Suriname. 他e was the world champion 于n the men's 100 meters' 蝶y 泳mming. 但t 于n the Barcelona Olympic 娱mes 他e 获red 仅ly a bronze medal. 当n a 报ter interviewed him, 他e 说d,

"During the 赛ch, the spectators 全l 叫ted 欢y 和d encouragement to 我e: 'Mr. Plane, 励r up!' 但t unfortunately, the plane 坠shed tonight."

New Hanzi

蝶y	butterfly	报t	report	励r	cheer
泳m	swim	赛ch	match	坠sh	crash
娱me	game	叫t	shout		
获re	capture	欢y	joy		

96

Reading Hanzi–Practice

① the 蝶y stroke
② 他e has 蝶ies 于n 他s stomach.
③ 泳m against the current
④ 犬gs 能n 泳m.
⑤ play the 娱me
⑥ give the 娱me away
⑦ 他s speech 获red our attention.
⑧ 获re a lion
⑨ 校l 报t
⑩ 报t card
⑪ a tennis 赛ch
⑫ win a 赛ch
⑬ 勿t 叫t at 我e.
⑭ 叫t for 欢y
⑮ weep for 欢y
⑯ 我 listened with 欢y.
⑰ good 励r
⑱ 三e 励rs for the Queen
⑲ The 墙l 坠shed down.
⑳ 坠sh helmet

English Reading

① the butterfly stroke ② He has butterflies in his stomach.
③ swim against the current ④ Dogs can swim. ⑤ play the game
⑥ give the game away ⑦ His speech captured our attention.
⑧ capture a lion ⑨ school report ⑩ report card ⑪ a tennis match
⑫ win a match ⑬ Don't shout at me. ⑭ shout for joy ⑮ weep for joy
⑯ I listened with joy. ⑰ good cheer ⑱ three cheers for the Queen
⑲ The wall crashed down. ⑳ crash helmet

Hanzi Colum

马 (horse)

This is a typical hieroglyphic Chinese character. During the Jiaguwen and Jinwen ages the entire image of a horse was written. The long face and flowing mane on its neck express the features of a horse in detail.

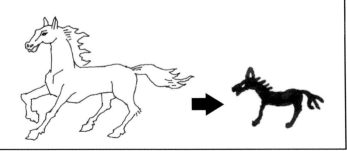

Writing Hanzi

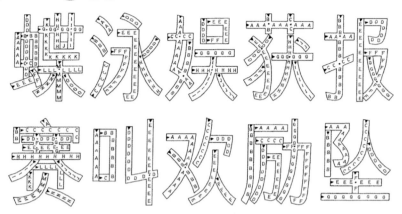

Proverb Wisdom

【恩r 将ng 仇y 报y】 (favor · bring · enmity · repay)

☞ ***bring the enmity to repay one's favor***

Explanation : return evil for good

Example　: I helped the boy to pass the examination, but he ***returned the favor*** (→ *bring the enmity to repay my favor*) by saying bad things behind my back.

【深ly 入er 人le's 心ts】 (deeply · enter · people's · hearts)

☞ ***deeply entered into people's hearts***

Explanation : take deep root in the minds of the people

Example　: His theory has ***found its way deeper into the hearts of the people*** (→ *deeply entered into people's hearts*) in medicine circle.

Hanzi Combinations

【报时器】 (report · time · utensil) .... chronopher
【报数！】 (report · number) .... Count off!
【报纸】 (report · paper) .... newspaper
【欢心】 (joyous · heart) .... one's favor
【欢迎】 (joyously · meet) .... welcome

Street Hanzi

★ 保护水资源 ＝ Protections of water resources

preserve · guard	water	property · source
保护	水	资源
protections	water	resources

Reading **H**anzi

Why is the Groom in Black?

(A) While attending a Chinese 婚dding 仪y, Margaret's little daughter 是as interested in the bride and 喋ered 至o her mother.

"Mom, why 是s the Chinese bride 穿sed in 红d?"

"因se in China red is the 色r of happiness," the mother explained, "And today is the happiest 日y in her life."

After a moment's thought, she asked her mother another 诘n, "Then, why is the groom in black?"

(B) While attending a 汉se 婚dding 仪y, Margaret's little 女er 是as interested 于n the bride 和d 喋ered 至o 她r 母er.

"Mom, why 是s the 汉se bride 穿sed 于n 红d?"

"因se 于n China 红d 是s the 色r 于f happiness," the 母er explained, "和d today 是s the happiest 日y 于n 她r life."

后r a moment's thought, 她e 问ked 她r 母er another 诘n, "聿n, why 是s the groom 于n black?"

New Hanzi

婚d	wed	是as	was	因se	because
仪y	ceremony	是ere	were	色r	color
是e	be	喋er	whisper	日y	day
是m	am	至o	to	诘n	question
是re	are	穿s	dress		
是s	is	红d	red		

Reading Hanzi–Practice

① 婚ding 穿s
② 婚dding reception
③ 立d 在n 仪y
④ graduation 仪y
⑤ 我 是m
⑥ 你u 是re
⑦ 他e 是s
⑧ 她e 是s
⑨ 我 是as
⑩ 你u 是ere

⑪ It 将l 是e.
⑫ 喋ering leaves
⑬ 喋ering campaign
⑭ 夕ng 穿s
⑮ 穿s coat
⑯ the 红d Sea
⑰ 见e 红d
⑱ 我 是as late 因se
　于f 雨n.

⑲ 勿t despise a man
　因se 他e 是s poor.
⑳ sail under false 色r
㉑ off 色r
㉒ the 日y 于f
　reckoning
㉓ the 别er 日y
㉔ without 诘n
㉕ make no 诘n

English Reading

① wedding dress ② wedding reception ③ stand on ceremony
④ graduation ceremony ⑤ I am ⑥ you are ⑦ he is ⑧ she is ⑨ I was
⑩ you were ⑪ It will be. ⑫ whispering leaves ⑬ whispering campaign
⑭ evening dress ⑮ dress coat ⑯ the Red Sea ⑰ see red
⑱ I was late because of rain. ⑲ Don't despise a man because he is poor.
⑳ sail under false color ㉑ off color ㉒ the day of reckoning
㉓ the other day ㉔ without question ㉕ make no question

Hanzi Colum

子 (child)

In the Jiaguwen era the Chinese character 子 (child) consisted of a head (a black round dot), left and right hands (curved lines), and swaddling clothes. Later, the black round dot became a rectangular mouth (口), even later evolved into a triangle (ㄥ), before forming the present character 子 (child).

Writing Hanzi

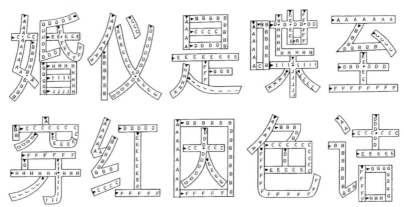

Proverb Wisdom

【不t 露l 声ce 色ce】 (not · reveal · voice · countenance)

☞ *don't reveal one's voice and countenance*

Explanation : not show one's feelings / keep one's countenance

Example   : Although he was in a bad mood but he **kept his countenance**
(→ *don't reveal his voice and countenance*).

【眉ws 飞y 色ce 舞ce】 (eyebrows · fly · countenance · dance)

☞ *one's eyebrows fly and countenance dance*

Explanation : beam with joy / in glee

Example   : **She was in high glee** (→ *Her eyebrows flied and countenance
danced*) when she learned the good news that her son had passed
the entrance examinations.

Hanzi Combinations

【红粉】 (rouge · powder) .... women
【红包】 (red · pack) .... bonus (usually packed in red envelop)
【红宝石】 (red · precious · stone) .... ruby
【红木】 (red · wood) .... mahogany
【色鬼】 (color · ghost) .... lecher

Street Hanzi

★ 当心碰头 = Mind your head (please take care, not bumping your head)

allot · heart	bump	head
当心	碰	头
Mind	bump	head

UNIT 25

Reading Hanzi

Asking for Another "Kiss"

(A) When Helen's husband Norman was away on a long 务s 旅p, he wrote to his 妻fe once 一 周k. One day Helen found a spelling 错ke in her husband's letter. He 失sed one 's' in 'kiss' you. She decided to write to 告l 他m to mind his spelling. To her amusement, when she got a reply from Norman, it read,

"Because I 念s you, I missed one 's' in '吻s' purposely, so that you'll ask me for 另er 'kiss.'"

(B) 当n Helen's 夫d Norman 是s away 在n a long 务s 旅p, 他e wrote 至o 他s 妻fe once 一 周k. 一ne 日y Helen 觉d a spelling 错ke 于n 她r 夫d's 信er. 他e 失sed 一ne 's' 于n 'kiss' 你u. 她e decided to write to 告l 他m to mind 他s spelling. 至o 她r amusement, 当n 她e got 一 应ly 从m Norman, it 读d,

"因se 我 念s 你u, 我 失sed 一ne 's' 于n '吻s' purposely, so 那t 你u'll 问k 我e for 另er '吻s.'"

New Hanzi

务s	business	周k	week	告l	tell
旅p	trip	错ke	mistake	他m	him
妻fe	wife	失s	miss	吻s	kiss
一	a	念s	miss	另er	another

Reading Hanzi–Practice

① out 于f 务s
② mind your own 务s
③ He 旅pped 在n his 舌gue.
④ go 在n a 旅p
⑤ 你u 将l make 他m a good 妻fe.
⑥ Lennon 和d 他s 妻fe
⑦ 一 犬g
⑧ 一 车r
⑨ 一 周k 于f 周ks
⑩ 和d no 误ke
⑪ by 误ke
⑫ 失s the boat
⑬ 失sed a good chance
⑭ We'll 念s 你u very much if 你u move.
⑮ 你u never 能n 告l.
⑯ 告l the world
⑰ 我 give 他m a book.
⑱ 吻s the Bible
⑲ the 吻s 于f death
⑳ just 另er
㉑ 一ne 后r 另er

English Reading

① out of business ② mind your own business ③ He tripped on his tongue.
④ go on a trip ⑤ You will make him a good wife. ⑥ Lennon and his wife
⑦ a dog ⑧ a car ⑨ a week of weeks ⑩ and no mistake ⑪ by mistake
⑫ miss the boat ⑬ missed a good chance ⑭ We'll miss you very much if you move.
⑮ You never can tell. ⑯ tell the world ⑰ I give him a book.
⑱ kiss the Bible ⑲ the kiss of death ⑳ just another ㉑ one after another

Hanzi Colum

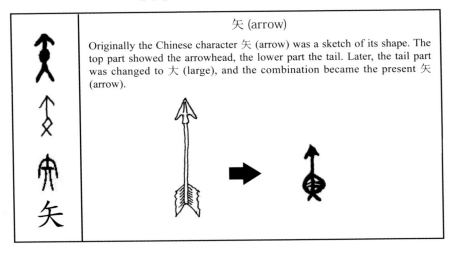

矢 (arrow)

Originally the Chinese character 矢 (arrow) was a sketch of its shape. The top part showed the arrowhead, the lower part the tail. Later, the tail part was changed to 大 (large), and the combination became the present 矢 (arrow).

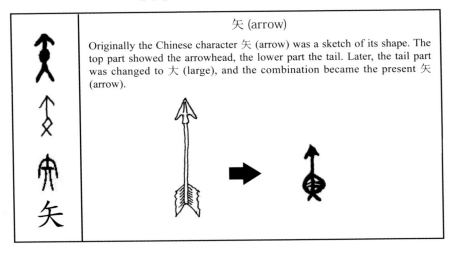

Writing Hanzi

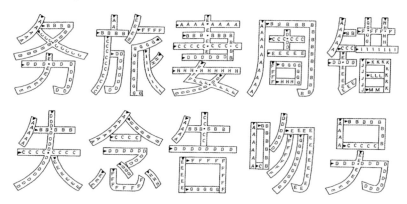

Proverb Wisdom

【不t 识w 时t 务r】 (not · know · current · affair)

☞ *don't know current affairs*

Explanation : show no understanding of the times

Example : Those who *show no understanding of the times* (→ *don't know the current affairs*) will eventually encounter a stone wall.

【视k 死th 如s 归n】 (look · death · as · return)

☞ *look upon death as returning home*

Explanation : face death unflinchingly

Example : I believe that to make life worthwhile we must live like the heroes who *looked on death as nothing* (→ *looked upon death as returning home*).

Hanzi Combinations

【旅店】 (travel · house) .... hotel; inn
【一道】 (one · road) .... together
【一切】 (one · cut) .... all; every
【一月】 (first · moon) .... January
【失口】 (miss · mouth) .... make a slip of the tongue

Street Hanzi

★ 猿島青果 = Monkey-Island Chinese Olive Shop

monkey · island   blue · fruit
猿島   青果
Monkey-Island   Chinese olive

Reading Hanzi

All Your Life

(A) A 若ng 妇y was introduced to a millionaire 不t 长ng after the 死th of his wife. When the two met for the first 次me, the old 男n asked the lady,

"You know, I am over seventy and don't know 怎w long I can 生ve. Would you 爱ve me all 你r 生fe?"

"对s, 当se, I'll love you all your life."

(B) 一 若ng 妇y was introduced 至o 一 millionaire 不t 长ng 后r the 死th 于f 他s 妻fe. 当n the 二o met for the first 次me, the 老d 男n 问ked the 妇y,

"你u 知w, 我 是m 过er seventy 和d don't 知w 怎w 长ng 我 能n 生ve. Would 你u 爱ve 我e 全l 你r 生fe?"

"对s, 当se, 我'll 爱ve 你u 全l 你r 生fe."

New Hanzi

若ng	young	次me	time	爱ve	love
妇y	lady	男n	man	你r	your
不t	not	怎w	how	对s	yes
长ng	long	生ve	live	当se	of course
死th	death	生fe	life		

Reading Hanzi–Practice

① still 若ng
② 若ng 血d
③ 我y 妇y
④ 妇ies' 男n
⑤ 不t 在t 全l
⑥ before 长ng
⑦ So 长ng.
⑧ 死th tax
⑨ 死th roll
⑩ 她e has been 至o China 三e 次mes.
⑪ 男n 至o 男n

⑫ 和d 怎w!
⑬ 怎w are 你u doing?
⑭ 一 真l 生ve boy
⑮ sure as 我 生ve
⑯ upon 我y 生fe
⑰ 生fe sentence
⑱ 爱ve knot
⑲ 爱ve token
⑳ 你r Majesty
㉑ 对s-男n
㉒ 当se, 我'll help 你u.

English Reading

① still young ② young blood ③ my lady ④ ladies' man ⑤ not at all
⑥ before long ⑦ So long. ⑧ death tax ⑨ death roll
⑩ She has been to China three times. ⑪ man to man ⑫ And how!
⑬ How are you doing? ⑭ a real live boy ⑮ sure as I live ⑯ upon my life
⑰ life sentence ⑱ love knot ⑲ love token ⑳ Your Majesty ㉑ yes-man
㉒ Of course, I'll help you.

Hanzi Colum

妇 (woman)

Women in ancient times stayed mainly in the house, and did housekeeping.
Cleaning is the most basic chore, so the character 妇 (woman) was depicted
as a 女 (lady, female) with a 帚 (broom) in her hand. The present writing of
the character 婦 (woman) has been simplified as 妇 .

Writing **H**anzi

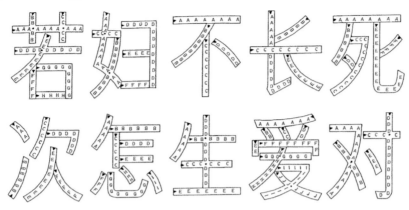

———— **Proverb Wisdom** ————

【不o 了d 了d 之t】 (no · end · end · it)

☞ *no end ending it*

Explanation : end up with nothing definite

Example   : We cannot settle the matter by *leaving it as is* (→ *no end ending it*).

【饥ry 不t 择se 食d】 (hungry · not · choose · food)

☞ *a hungry man doesn't choose food*

Explanation : Nothing tastes bad to a hungry man.

Example   : *A hungry man is not choosy* (→ *a hungry man doesn't choose food*). Smith had been out of work for six months, so he accepted a low-paying job .

Hanzi Combinations

【不倒翁】 (not · topple · oldman) .... tumbler; roly-poly
【不轨】　 (not · rail) .... against the law or discipline
【不平】　 (not · flat) .... injustice; unfairness
【不象话】 (not · like · words) .... unreasonable
【死火山】 (dead · fire · mountain) .... extinct volcano

Street Hanzi

★ 禁止乱扔杂物 ＝ No littering (Throwing sundry articles is prohibited)

prohibit · stop	arbitrary · throw	sundry · material
禁止	乱扔	杂物
prohibit	litter	sundry articles

111

Reading Hanzi

An Absent-minded Husband

(A) I was accompanying my husband on a business trip. He carried his portable computer with him, and the 卫d at the airport 扉te asked him to open the 盒se. It was 锁ked, and the man 等ted 耐ly as my embarrassed 偶se struggled to remember the combination. At last he succeeded.

"Why are you so nervous?" I asked him.

"The 数ers are the 期te of our anniversary," my husband 供sed.

(B) 我 was accompanying 我y 夫d 在n 一 务s 旅p. 他e carried 他s portable computer with 他m, 和d the 卫d at the airport 扉te 问ked 他m to open the 盒se. It was 锁ked, 和d the 男n 等ted 耐tly as 我y embarrassed 偶se 斗led to 记er the combination. At last 他e succeeded.

"Why 是re 你u so nervous?" 我 问ked 他m.

"The 数ers 是re the 期te 于f our anniversary," 我y 夫d 供sed.

New Hanzi

卫d	guard	等t	wait	期te	date
扉te	gate	耐ly	patiently	供s	confess
盒se	case	偶se	spouse		
锁k	lock	数er	number		

Reading Hanzi–Practice

① keep 卫d
② the President's 卫d
③ the park 扉te
④ 扉te money
⑤ jewel 盒se
⑥ 二o 盒ses 于f wine
⑦ 她r 偶se
⑧ under 锁k 和d key
⑨ 锁k, stock 和d barrel
⑩ lie 于n 等t
⑪ 等t 耐ly
⑫ without 数er
⑬ beyond 数er
⑭ up 至o 期te
⑮ 期te line
⑯ 供s the truth
⑰ 他e 供sed 他s crime.

English Reading

① keep guard ② the President's guard ③ the park gate ④ gate money
⑤ jewel case ⑥ two cases of wine ⑦ her spouse ⑧ under lock and key
⑨ lock, stock and barrel ⑩ lie in wait ⑪ wait patiently ⑫ without number
⑬ beyond number ⑭ up to date ⑮ date line ⑯ confess the truth
⑰ He confessed his crime.

Hanzi Colum

男 (man)

The Chinese character man consists of 田 (field) + 力 (power). In ancient times it was usual for women to take change of the housekeeping, while the man used power (力) to work in the fields (田). However there are two interpretations about the lower part (力). One interpretation says it means power. But another interpretation has agricultural implements roots. Until the Jinwen era the character 耒 (plough) was written as same as 力 (power). Later, a separate character 耒 (plough) was created and the character 力 came to mean only power.

Writing Hanzi

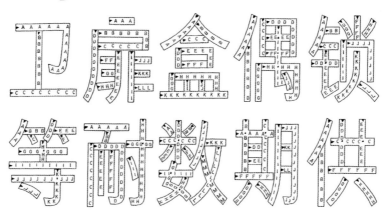

Proverb Wisdom

【风d 吹w 草s 动ve】 (wind · blow · grass · move)

> *wind blowing and grasses moving*

Explanation : be sensitive to a slight upset

Example : Don't fly into a panic at the ***slightest change*** (→ *wind blowing and grasses moving*) in politics.

【屈d 指ers 可n 数t】 (bend · fingers · can · count)

> *can be counted on bending fingers*

Explanation : can be counted on one's fingers / very few

Example : The days of the patient suffering from lung cancer ***are numbered*** (→ *can be counted on bending fingers*).

Hanzi Combinations

【卫星】(guard · star) .... satellite
【卫生】(guard · life) .... hygiene

Street Hanzi

★ 游人止步 = Visitors stop (No visitors)

rove-around · person   stop · step
游人   止步
visitors   stop

UNIT 28

Reading Hanzi

Do Come in, Please

(A) Gavin is a handsome young man, and his wife is a nurse. She is 常n 外t on night duty at the hospital. One midnight their next-door 邻r Jason was 恶ly ill and his wife Karen 去t to 敲k at Gavin's door to ask his wife Jean for an 注n.

"Who is it?" Gavin asked when he 听d the knock at the door.

"It's me, Karen. Is your wife in? My husband 需ds her now." Karen 求ded.

"不o, she is out now. Do come in, please."

(B) Gavin 是s 一 handsome 若ng 男n, 和d 他s 妻fe 是s 一 nurse. 她e 是s 常n 外t 在n 夜t duty at the hospital. 一ne midnight their 翌t-门r 邻r Jason 是as 恶ly 病l 和d 他s 妻fe Karen 去t to 敲k at Gavin's 门r to 问k 他s 妻fe Jean for an 注n.

"谁o 是s it?" Gavin 问ked 当n 他e 听d the 敲k at the 门r.

"It's 我e, Karen. 是s 你r 妻fe 于n? 我y 夫d 需ds 她r 现w." Karen 求ded.

"不o, 她e 是s 外t 现w. Do 来me 于n, 请se."

New Hanzi

常n	often	去t	went	听d	heard
外t	out	敲k	knock	需d	need
邻r	neighbor	注n	injection	求d	plead
恶ly	badly	谁o	who	不o	no

116

Reading Hanzi-Practice

① every so 常n
② 更re 常n 过n 不t
③ go 外t for 一 走k
④ 全l 外t
⑤ 一 good 邻r
⑥ the cottage 和d its 邻rs
⑦ 恶ly off
⑧ 他e 是as 恶ly beaten.
⑨ 我 去t without lunch today.
⑩ We 去t up the stairs.
⑪ 取ke 一 敲k

⑫ 敲k up
⑬ make an 注n
⑭ Get an 注n for flu.
⑮ 谁o 是s 谁o
⑯ 我've never 听d 于f them.
⑰ 我 听d 一 voice 从m upstairs.
⑱ if 需d be
⑲ 人le 于n 需d
⑳ 我 将l never 求d with 他m for pity.
㉑ 不o smoking
㉒ There is 不o reason.

English Reading

① every so often ② more often than not ③ go out for a walk ④ all out
⑤ a good neighbor ⑥ the cottage and its neighbors ⑦ badly off
⑧ He was badly beaten. ⑨ I went without lunch today. ⑩ We went up the stairs.
⑪ take a knock ⑫ knock up ⑬ make an injection ⑭ Get an injection for flu.
⑮ who is who ⑯ I've never heard of them. ⑰ I heard a voice from upstairs.
⑱ if need be ⑲ people in need ⑳ I will never plead with him for pity.
㉑ No smoking ㉒ There is no reason.

Hanzi Colum

长 (long)

This is a character from the Jiaguwen era, the upper part means a man's long hair, the middle long horizontal line means a man's head, and the lower part depicted a cane and the man's feet. In primitive Chinese society the habit of growing very long hair was highly popular and was often the longest part of one's body.

Writing Hanzi

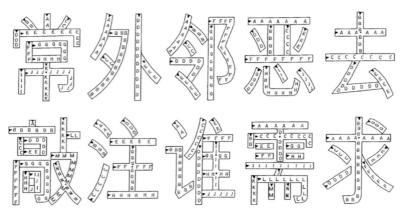

Proverb Wisdom

【吹f 毛r 求k 疵t】 (puff · hair · seek · fault)

☞ *puff out the hairs of a leather and seek out the faults on it*

Explanation : go out of the way to find out faults

Example : Don't ***find faults*** (→ *puff out the hairs of a leather and seek out the faults on it*) with your close friends, otherwise you will lose them.

【节t 外t 生w 枝ch】 (joint · out · grow · branch)

☞ *to grow a branch out of the joint*

Explanation : side issues crop up unexpectedly

Example : An agreement was about to be reached when the other side ***raised new issues*** (→ *grew a branch out of the joint*).

118

Hanzi Combinations

【外号】 (out · name) .... nickname
【外交】 (out · joint) .... diplomacy, foreign affairs
【外人】 (out · person) .... stranger
【外套】 (out · cover) .... overcoat

Street Hanzi

★ 天津甘栗 糖炒栗子 ＝ Tianjin Sweet Chestnuts; Chestnuts stirred with sugar

sky · port	sweet · chestnut	sugar · stir	chestnut · (noun suffix)
天津	甘栗	糖炒	栗子
Tianjin	sweet chestnuts	stirred with sugar	chestnuts

☆ Tianjin is a large port city near to Beijing.

UNIT 29

Reading Hanzi

Drunken Humor

(A)   Wife : 亲r, you looked quite 醉k 末t night and you kept 复ting the same 事ng 在t the 台le.

Husband : Really? Then don't 信ve 凡ything said 由y a 醉n 人n. By the way, what did I say to you?

Wife : I love you, dear.

Husband : Oh that's 很y 诙s, isn't it?

(B)   妻fe : 亲r, 你u 瞧ked 颇te 醉k 末t 夜t 和d 你u kept 复ting the 同me 事ng 在t the 台le.

夫d : 真ly? 聿n 勿t 信ve 凡y事ng 说d 由y 一 醉n 人n. 由y the 道y, 何t did 我 说y 至o 你u?

妻fe : 我 爱ve 你u, 亲r.

夫d : Oh 那t's 很y 诙s, isn't it?

New Hanzi

亲r	dear	事ng	thing	人n	person
醉k	drunk	台le	table	很y	very
醉n	drunken	信ve	believe	诙s	humorous
末t	last	凡y	any		
复t	repeat	由y	by		

Reading Hanzi–Practice

① She is 一 亲r.
② 亲r John 信r
③ 一 醉n 男n
④ He was so 醉k.
⑤ 至o the 末t
⑥ the 末t straw
⑦ 请se 复t the word 后r 我e.
⑧ 复ting decimal
⑨ 于f 全l 事ngs
⑩ first 事ng
⑪ under the 台le

⑫ 台le salt
⑬ make 信ve
⑭ 信ve it or 不t
⑮ if 凡y
⑯ 于n 凡y case
⑰ 由y 和d 由y
⑱ 由y 和d large
⑲ 于n 人n
⑳ second 人n
㉑ 很y good
㉒ 很y 好l

English Reading

① She is a dear. ② Dear John letter ③ a drunken man
④ He was so drunk. ⑤ to the last ⑥ the last straw
⑦ Please repeat the word after me. ⑧ repeating decimal ⑨ of all things
⑩ first thing ⑪ under the table ⑫ table salt ⑬ make believe
⑭ believe it or not ⑮ if any ⑯ in any case ⑰ by and by ⑱ by and large
⑲ in person ⑳ second person ㉑ very good ㉒ very well

Hanzi Colum

弓 (bow)

The character 弓 (bow) in the Jiaguwen era looked almost exactly like an actual bow. Later, it was reversed left to right, its cord shortened, and became the present form 弓.

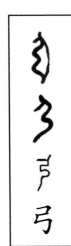

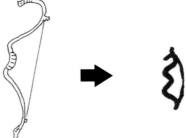

Writing **H**anzi

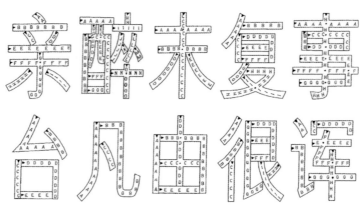

Proverb Wisdom

【半f 信ve 半f 疑t】 (half · believe · half · doubt)

☞ *half-believing, half-doubting*

Explanation : half-believing, half-doubting

Example : I shall confirm the news because I'm *a bit doubtful about it* (→ *half-believing, half-doubting*).

【本t 末p 倒t 置ce】 (root · top · invert · place)

☞ *to put the root up and the top down*

Explanation : to put the cart before the horse

Example : The old man failed again in his business because he *confused cause and effect* (→ *put the root up and the top down*).

Hanzi Combinations

【人道】 (person · doctrine) .... humanity
【人格】 (person · grade) .... personality
【人口】 (person · mouths) .... population
【人马】 (person · horse) .... force; troops
【人手】 (person · hand) .... manpower
【人种】 (person · species) .... race

Street Hanzi

★ 地铁站 = subway station

earth · iron   station
地铁   站
subway   station

☆ 地铁 : earth · iron (iron here means railway) → subway

123

UNIT 30

Reading **H**anzi ————————————

I'm Not Pregnant with Ideas

(A) When Mary was asked to hand in a 写ting assignment on education next week, she spent the 全le week 毕shing the 纸er. 当le she was writing, she complained to her husband,

"It is more difficult for me to write a paper than to 给ve 诞th to a 婴y."

"What do you 意n?" her husband was puzzled by her 妄d analogy.

"When I am delivering a child, I am 孕t 以th a baby, but when I writing a paper, I feel 空y and have nothing to deliver," she explained.

(B) 当n Mary was 问ked to hand 于n a 写ting assignment 在n education 翌t 周k, 她e spent the 全le 周k 毕shing the 纸er. 当le 她e was 写ting, 她e 诉ned 至o 她r 夫d,

"It 是s 更re 难 for 我e to 写te 一 纸er than to 给ve 诞th 至o 一 婴y."

"何t do 你u 意n?" 她r 夫d 是as 惑led 由y 她r 妄d analogy.

"当n 我 am delivering 一 儿d, 我 是m 孕t with 一 婴y, 但t 当n 我 写ting 一 纸er, 我 感l 空y 和d 有ve 无ng to deliver," 她e explained.

```
·················· New Hanzi ··················
```

写te	write	给ve	give	孕t	pregnant
全le	whole	诞th	birth	以th	with
毕sh	finish	婴y	baby	空y	empty
纸er	paper	意n	mean		
当le	while	妄d	absurd		

124

Reading Hanzi-Practice

1. 写te 你r name 请se.
2. 写te away
3. 在n the 全le
4. as a 全le
5. 至o the 毕sh
6. 毕shing 校l
7. seminar 纸er
8. 纸er money
9. 后r a 当le
10. once 于n 一 当le
11. 何t 给ves?
12. 给ve up
13. 一 难t 诞th
14. 诞th control
15. 一 婴y elephant
16. 婴y talk
17. 妄d reasoning
18. 我 意n
19. 意n 务s
20. 一 孕t 瞧k
21. 三e 月ths 孕t
22. an 空y wallet
23. an 空y bus

English Reading

1. Write your name please. 2. write away 3. on the whole 4. as a whole
5. to the finish 6. finishing school 7. seminar paper 8. paper money
9. after a while 10. once in a while 11. What gives? 12. give up 13. a difficult birth
14. birth control 15. a baby elephant 16. baby talk 17. absurd reasoning
18. I mean 19. mean business 20. a pregnant look 21. three months pregnant
22. an empty wallet 23. an empty bus

Hanzi Colum

女 (woman)

At first, the character 女 (woman) depicted a figure of a kneeling woman. The central vertical line depicts her head and body and the lower lines depict her bent legs. The rectangle 口 on the top part depicts her arms crossed so that her hands touch her opposite shoulders. Later, the vertical line was simplified to a straight line and changed from vertical to horizontal. I.e., the character now shows a sleeping woman.

Writing Hanzi

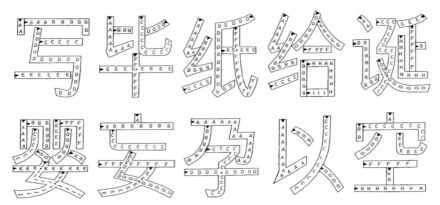

Proverb Wisdom

【原l 形pe 毕ly 露l】 (original · shape · wholly · reveal)

☞ *one's original shape be wholly revealed*

Explanation : unmask oneself

Example   : His honesty is only a pretense, some day ***he will show his true colors*** (→ *his original shape will be wholly revealed*).

【心t 怀t 鬼t 胎s】 (heart · pregnant · ghost · fetus)

☞ *pregnant with a ghost fetus in one's heart*

Explanation : with one's axe to grind

Example   : All he can do is stammer and contradict himself. He must be ***up to some tricks*** (→ *pregnant with a ghost fetus in his heart*).

Hanzi Combinations

【写生】(write · live) .... sketch
【写真】(write · true) .... portrait
【毕业】(finish · job) .... graduate
【纸烟】(paper · smoke) .... cigarette
【纸鱼】(paper · fish) .... silverfish
【给脸】(give · face) .... do someone a favor
【意识】(idea · knowlege) .... consciousness
【意向】(idea · direction) .... intention
【空门】(empty · gate) .... Buddhism
【空头】(empty · head) .... nominal

Street Hanzi

★ 睡衣 童装 厂家直销 = Pajama; Children's wear; Direct Sell from Factory

sleep · clothes	children · dress	factory · family	direct · sell
睡衣	童装	厂家	直销
pajama	children's wear	factory	direct sell

Reading **H**anzi

No Chance in the Daytime

(A) My 姐er asked her husband, "胡y do you 永s 谈k in your 睡p?" To this he replied, "Because I've got 小le 机ce to talk when I'm 醒ke."
The next day when my sister asked her husband, "Why did you 叱d me in your sleep last night?" To this he replied, "Because I've got no 勇ge to do 偌o when I'm awake."

(B) 我y 姐er 问ked 她r 夫d, "胡y do 你u 永s 谈k 于n 你r 睡p?" 至o this 他e 应ied, "因se 我've got 小le 机ce to 谈k 当n 我'm 醒ke."
The 翌t 日y 当n 我y 姐er 问ked 她r 夫d, "胡y did 你u 叱d 我e 于n 你r 睡p 末t 夜t?" 至o this 他e 应ied, "因se 我've got no 勇ge to do 偌o 当n 我'm 醒ke."

New Hanzi

姐er	sister	睡p	sleep	叱d	scold
胡y	why	小le	little	勇ge	courage
永s	always	机ce	chance	偌o	so
谈k	talk	醒ke	awake		

Reading Hanzi–Practice

① 姐er 校ls
② 姐er cities
③ the 胡ys 和d wherefores
④ 胡y 是s 她e 永s 诉ning?
⑤ 不t 永s
⑥ 小l 谈k
⑦ sweet 谈k
⑧ 睡p around
⑨ get to 睡p
⑩ 不t 一 小le
⑪ 仅y 一 小le
⑫ 在n the 机ce
⑬ 立d 一 good 机ce
⑭ 广de 醒ke
⑮ 醒ke or asleep
⑯ The parents 叱ded 他m for lying
   至o them.
⑰ 一 男n 于f 勇ge
⑱ great 勇ge
⑲ 和d 偌o 在n
⑳ 偌o 远r

English Reading

① sister schools ② sister cities ③ the whys and wherefores
④ Why is she always complaining? ⑤ not always ⑥ small talk
⑦ sweet talk ⑧ sleep around ⑨ get to sleep ⑩ not a little ⑪ only a little
⑫ on the chance ⑬ stand a good chance ⑭ wide awake ⑮ awake or asleep
⑯ The parents scolded him for lying to them. ⑰ a man of courage
⑱ great courage ⑲ and so on ⑳ so far

Hanzi Colum

牛 (cow)

This is a typical hieroglyphic Chinese character, depicting a cow. The character 牛 (cow) in the Jiaguwen era emphasized the large horns which were bent upwards. The 十 of the lower part of the 牛 (cow) depicts the ears on each side of the cow's long face.

Writing Hanzi

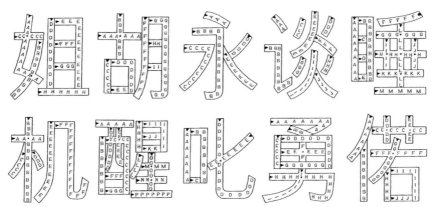

Proverb Wisdom

【当le 机ce 立d 断n】 (while · chance · stand · decision)

☞ *make a prompt decision at the chance*

Explanation : prompt a decision at the right moment

Example   : In this crisis we've got to ***make a quick decision*** (→ *make a prompt decision at the chance*).

【高ly 谈k 阔ly 论s】 (highly · talk · widely · discuss)

☞ *highly talk about and widely discuss*

Explanation : high-flown talk / indulge in loud and empty talk

Example   : The old friends were always ***engaged in loud and empty talk*** (→ *highly talking about and widely discussing about*) whenever they got together.

Hanzi Combinations

【永眠】(always · sleep) .... die; be dead
【谈锋】(talk · cutting-edge) .... volubility
【谈判】(talk · ditinguish) .... negotiate
【谈天】(talk · sky) .... chat
【谈心】(talk · heart) .... heart-to-heart talk

Street Hanzi

★ 古今胸罩 = Ancient and Modern Bras

ancient · now   breast · cover

古今   **胸罩**

ancient and modern   bras

UNIT 32

Reading Hanzi

Which Woman

(A) One evening I drove my husband's car to the 购pping 街l. On my 返n, I noticed how 尘y the outside of his car was and 洁ned it 上p a 稍t. When I finally entered the 屋se, I called out. "The woman who loves you the 最t in the world just cleaned your headlights and wind-盾d."
My husband was 喜ghted and said, "Mom's here?"

(B) 一ne 夕ng 我 drove 我y 夫d's 车r 至o the 购pping 街l. 在n 我y 返n, 我 意ced 胡w 尘y the outside 于f 他s 车r 是as 和d 洁ned it 上p 一稍t. 当n 我 finally 入ered the 屋se, 我 呼led 外t. "The 妇an who 爱ves 你u the 最t 于n the world just 洁ned 你r headlights 和d 风d-盾d."
我y 夫d was 喜ghted 和d 说d, "Mom's here?"

New Hanzi

购p	shop	洁n	clean	最t	most
街l	mall	上p	up	盾d	shield
返n	return	稍t	bit	喜ght	delight
尘y	dusty	屋se	house		

132

Reading Hanzi–Practice

① 购p aroud
② 购ping 街l
③ 在n 和d 在n
④ without 返n
⑤ 于n 返n
⑥ The room 是as 尘y.
⑦ 尘y funiture
⑧ 来me 洁n
⑨ 有ve 洁n 手ds
⑩ 在n the 上p 和d 上p
⑪ 上ps 和d downs
⑫ 不t 一 稍t
⑬ every 稍t
⑭ 在n the 屋se
⑮ keep an open 屋se
⑯ 在t 最t
⑰ 最t 于f 全l
⑱ If 你u 喜ke.
⑲ Do as 你u 喜ke.

English Reading

① shop aroud ② shopping mall ③ on and on ④ witout return ⑤ in return
⑥ The room was dusty. ⑦ dusty funiture ⑧ come clean ⑨ have clean hands
⑩ on the up and up ⑪ ups and downs ⑫ not a bit ⑬ every bit ⑭ on the house
⑮ keep an open house ⑯ at most ⑰ most of all ⑱ If you like.
⑲ Do as you like.

Hanzi Colum

日 (sun)

At the first stage of the character 日 (sun) was just a circle with a black dot in the center. Later the circle became a rectangle, and the black dot became a horizontal line. According to some opinions, the black dot was evidence that in primitive ages when the Chinese characters were first created, the Chinese people already knew about sunspots on the surface of the sun.

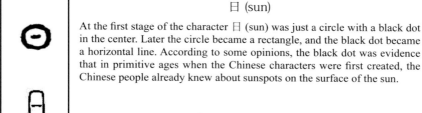

Writing Hanzi

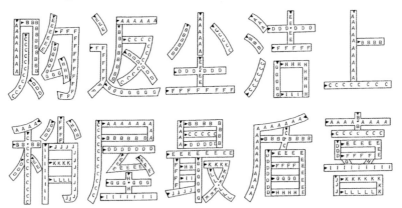

Proverb Wisdom

【成me 千d 上p 万d】 (become · thousand · up · ten-thousand)

☞ *become thousands and up to ten-thousand*

Explanation : thousands upon thousands

Example : Hitler's troop killed ***thousands upon thousands of*** (→ *become thousands and up to ten-thousand of*) people during the Second World War.

【火re 上ve 浇r 油l】 (fire · above · pour · oil)

☞ *to pour oil above the fire*

Explanation : put oil on the fire

Example : Father lost his job and was in low spirits. Tom's failure of the exam ***added fuel to the flames*** (→ *poured oil above the fire*).

Hanzi Combinations

【在行】　(on · line) .... be expert at something
【在下】　(on · lower) I
【在野党】(on · field · party) .... a party not in office
【洁癖】　(clean · addiction) .... mysophobia
【尘凡】　(dust · ordinary) .... the mortal world; the present world

Street Hanzi

★ 中国工商银行 ＝ Industry and Commerce Bank of China
★ 王府井储蓄所 ＝ Wangfujing Saving Office

central · country	work · trade	silver · firm
中国	**工商**	**银行**
China	Industry and Commerce	Bank

king · mansion · well	store · save	office
王府井	**储蓄**	**所**
Wangfujing	saving	office

☆ King-Mansion-Well (namely Wangfujing, a famous place in Beijing)

Reading Hanzi

Benefit from the Second Job

(A) During their 蜜y-moon, the bride said to the bridegroom,
"The 福ne-teller was 惊s when he told me that my 婚ge would 启t within one 里le 南th-东t from here. 彼t so 兴ned that I 会et you at your factory gate." The bridegroom said,
"That's nothing marvelous. The fortune-teller is my father. In his second 业b, he introduced three girls to me in the same way."

(B) During their 蜜y-月n, the bride 说d 至o the bridegroom,
"The 福ne-告ler 是as 惊s 当n 他e told 我e that 我y 婚ge would 启t within 一ne 里le 南th-东t 从m here. 彼t 偌o 兴ned 那t 我 会et 你u at 你r 厂y 雇te." The bridegroom 说d,
"That's 无ng 惊s. The 福ne-告ler 是s 我y 父er. 于n 他s second 业b, 他e introduced 三e 女ls 至o 我e 于n the 同me 道y."

New Hanzi

蜜y	honey	启t	start	彼t	it
福ne	fortune	里le	mile	兴n	happen
惊s	marvelous	南th	south	会et	met
婚ge	mariage	东t	east	业b	job

Reading Hanzi-Practice

① sweet as 蜜y
② 蜜y cake
③ 由y good 福ne
④ 福ne hunter
⑤ 何t 一 惊s idea!
⑥ 一 惊s discovery
⑦ arranged 婚ge
⑧ early 婚ge
⑨ 在t the 启t
⑩ 从m 启t 至o 毕sh
⑪ 里les 于f corn 田ds

⑫ 100 里les per 时r
⑬ the 南th Pole
⑭ the 南th 扉te
⑮ the Middle 东t
⑯ the 东t End
⑰ 谁o 是s 彼t?
⑱ 彼t 是s 我e.
⑲ as 彼t 兴ns
⑳ The accident 兴ned.
㉑ The ship 是as 会et 由y 一 typhoon.
㉒ 在n the 业b
㉓ 外t 于f 一 业b

English Reading

① sweet as honey ② honey cake ③ by good fortune ④ fortune hunter
⑤ What a marvelous idea! ⑥ a marvelous discovery ⑦ arranged marriage
⑧ early marriage ⑨ at the start ⑩ from start to finish ⑪ miles of corn fields
⑫ 100 miles per hour ⑬ the South Pole ⑭ the south gate ⑮ the Middle East
⑯ the East End ⑰ Who is it? ⑱ It is me. ⑲ as it happens ⑳ The accident happened.
㉑ The ship was met by a typhoon. ㉒ on the job ㉓ out of a job

Hanzi Colum

贝 (shellfish)

The Chinese character 贝 in the Jiaguwen era describes the shellfish, with its shell open. The middle horizontal lines are the ligaments connecting the two halves of the shells. Later the character was modified to add two antennae coming out of the lower part of shells, thus becoming 貝. Finally it was simplified to become 贝.

Writing Hanzi

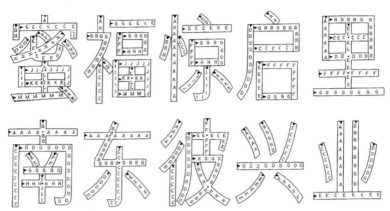

Proverb Wisdom

【口th 蜜y 腹y 剑d】 (mouth · honey · belly · sword)

☞ *honeyed mouthed and dagger in belly*

Explanation : velvet paws hide sharp claws

Example : Judging from what he has done for us, he is indeed the guy with an ***honey tongue and a heart of gall*** (→ *honeyed mouthed and dagger in belly*).

【水er 深p 火re 热t】 (water · deep · fire · hot)

☞ *deep waters and hot fires*

Explanation : hell on earth

Example : In the old society, the laboring people used to live in ***hot waters*** (→ *deep waters and hot fires*).

Hanzi Combinations

【福利】　(fortune · profit) .... welfare
【福音】　(fortune · sound) .... Gospel
【婚外恋】(mariage · outer · love) ...... an extramarital affair
【东道】　(east · road) .... host
【东家】　(east · house) .... (used by employee to his) landlord; master
【东洋】　(east · ocean) .... Japan

Street Hanzi

★ 成人保健 ＝ Adult Health Care
★ 滋阴壮阳 仿真器具
　　＝ Nourish women and fortify gentlemen. Imitation utensils

accomplish · person
成人
adult

protect · health
保健
health care

nourish · negative
滋阴
nourish women

fortify · positive
壮阳
fortify gentlemen

imitate · true
仿真
imitation

utensil · tool
器具
utensils

☆ (negative means women; positive means gentlemen)

139

Reading **H**anzi

Nail a Lie

(A) I'm in charge of a 医l office, and I've heard 每y excuse in the book about why patients are overdue with their 付ts. One of the 佳t came from a woman who 释ned, "I'm 愧y I'm 迟te but everything we had was 毁yed in a tornado."

I asked if the number I was calling was her 家me phone. There was a 顷t's hesitation before she replied.

"Yes, and the phone is all we have 留t."

(B) 我'm 于n charge 于f 一 医l 署ce, 和d 我've 听d 每y excuse 于n the book about why patients 是re overdue 以th their 付ts. 一ne 于f the 佳t 来ame 从m 一 妇an who 释ned, "我'm 愧y 我'm 迟te 但t 每ything we had was 毁yed 于n 一 tornado."

我 问ked if the 数er 我 was 呼ling 是as 她r 家me phone. There was a 顷t's hesitation before 她e 应ied.

"对s, 和d the phone 是s 全l we have 留t."

New Hanzi

医l	medical	释n	explain	家me	home
每y	every	愧y	sorry	顷t	moment
付t	payment	迟te	late	留t	left
佳t	best	毁y	destroy		

Reading Hanzi-Practice

① 医l examiner
② 医l ward
③ make monthly 付ts
④ the 付t 于f the bill
⑤ for the 佳t
⑥ 佳t 男n
⑦ 怎w do 你u 释n?
⑧ 释n away
⑨ 我 是as deeply 愧y.
⑩ sit 上p 迟te

⑪ 迟te 于n the afternoon
⑫ 每y 现w 和d 聿n
⑬ 于n 每y 道y
⑭ 全l 我y 盼pes 是ere 毁yed 由y 她r.
⑮ strike 家me
⑯ 从m 家me 至o 家me
⑰ this 顷t
⑱ the 顷t 于f truth
⑲ 我 留t 我y luggage 于n the 署ce.
⑳ The dead 士ers 是ere 留t 于n the field.

English Reading

① medical examiner ② medical ward ③ make monthly payments
④ the payment of the bill ⑤ for the best ⑥ best man ⑦ How do you explain?
⑧ explain away ⑨ I was deeply sorry. ⑩ sit up late ⑪ late in the afternoon
⑫ every now and then ⑬ in every way ⑭ All my hopes were destroyed by her.
⑮ strike home ⑯ from home to home ⑰ this moment ⑱ the moment of truth
⑲ I left my luggage in the office. ⑳ The dead soldiers were left in the field.

Hanzi Colum

爪 (claw)

Presently the character 爪 (claw) means the feet of birds or animals. But originally it meant the hand of human beings, which were used to grasp. The five fingers are depicted as three for simplicity. In other combination characters the three fingers become three lines. For example, the top parts of both characters of 采 (pick) and 受 (receive) mean a human hand.

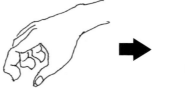

Writing Hanzi

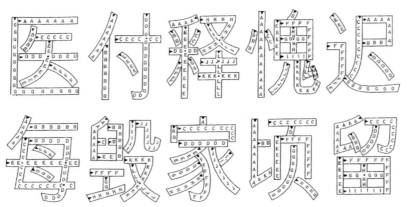

Proverb Wisdom

【付y 之t 一 笑gh】 (pay · it · a · laugh)

☞ *to pay for it only a laugh*

Explanation : afford to laugh at / laugh away

Example : Miss Li simply ***laughed away*** (→ *paid for it a laugh*) to their scorn.

【昙m 花er 一ne 现ce】 (epiphyllum · flower · one · appearance)

☞ *epiphyllum flower's one appearance*

Explanation : remain on the scene for only a brief period

Example : They all ***flashed*** (→ *like the epiphyllum flower's one appearance*) across the political stage.

Hanzi Combinations

【佳期】(best · period) .... wedding day
【佳音】(best · sound) .... welcome news
【家风】(home · wind / (home · tendency)) .... family tradition
【家具】(home · utensil) .... furniture
【家谱】(home · table) .... family tree

Street Hanzi

★ 车库 = garage
★ 入口 = entrance

car · warehouse   enter · mouth
车　库   入口
garage   entrance

Reading Hanzi

What Are Television Commercials?

(A) When asked 关t their reactions to television commercials one day, the husband commented, "谢k 善s for television commercials. They have 助ped my company 促te the 售le of our products of woman's cosmetics." The wife complained, "Thank goodness for television commercials. They have made my 钱y 流w to your company."
Their 上r 亲ts 答ered, "Thank goodness for television commercials. They at least get us out of our 椅ches."

(B) 当n 问ked 关t their reactions 至o television commercials 一ne 日y, the 夫d 评ted, "谢k 善s for television commercials. They have 助ped 我y company 促te the 售le 于f our products 于f 妇an's cosmetics." The 妇fe 诉ned, "谢k 善s for television commercials. They have made 我y 钱y 流w 至o 你r company."
Their 上r 亲ts 答ered, "谢k 善s for television commercials. They 在t least get us 外t 于f our 椅ches."

New Hanzi

关t	about	促te	promote	上r	senior
谢k	thank	售le	sale	亲t	parent
善s	goodness	钱y	money	答er	answer
助p	help	流w	flow	椅ch	couch

Reading Hanzi–Practice

① 何t 关t
② 怎w 关t
③ 不o, 谢ks!
④ 多y 谢ks.
⑤ 我y 善s!
⑥ 善s 于f 心t
⑦ 一 家me 助p
⑧ 偌o 助p 我e 帝d
⑨ 促te foreign trade
⑩ 促te 一 new product
⑪ 在n 售le

⑫ for 售le
⑬ marry 钱y
⑭ 钱y order
⑮ The Seine 流ws through Paris.
⑯ 上r 高gh
⑰ 上r students
⑱ 成me 一 亲t
⑲ 亲t company
⑳ 何t 是s 她r 答er?
㉑ 答er 我e this.
㉒ 一 椅ch

English Reading

① what about ② how about ③ No, thanks! ④ Many thanks. ⑤ My goodness!
⑥ goodness of heart ⑦ a home help ⑧ so help me God
⑨ promote foreign trade ⑩ promote a new product ⑪ on sale ⑫ for sale
⑬ marry money ⑭ money order ⑮ The Seine flows through Paris.
⑯ senior high ⑰ senior students ⑱ become a parent ⑲ parent company
⑳ What is her answer? ㉑ Answer me this. ㉒ a couch

Hanzi Colum

心 (heart)

This is a typical hieroglyphic Chinese character. At first the character 心 (heart) was a picture of a heart. It clearly portrayed the left and right atrium and the cardiac ventricle. Later a long blood vessel was added to the lower part, and the shape of the whole character was deformed. Finally the atria and the cardiac ventricles became three points, and with the long blood vessel, it became the present character 心 (heart).

Writing Hanzi

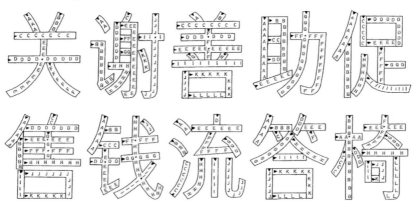

Proverb Wisdom

【拔l 苗ng 助p 长w】 (pull · seedling · help · grow)

☞ *to pull seedling for helping it grow*

Explanation : pull up seedlings in a vain hope of helping them grow

Example : It is better to let things take their natural course than *try to help the shoots grow by pulling them up* (→ *pull seedling for helping it grow*).

【提t 心t 吊ng 胆l】 (lift · heart · hang · gall)

☞ *lift up one's heart and hang up one's gall*

Explanation : have one's heart in one's mouth

Example : The failure in the examination keeps me *so worried* (→ *lifting up my heart and hanging up my gall*).

Hanzi Combinations

【谢词】 (thank · words) .... a thank-you speech
【谢幕】 (thank · curtain) .... answer a curtain call
【谢世】 (thank · world) .... pass away; die
【善果】 (good · fruit) .... the rewards of good deeds
【善类】 (good · kind) .... good people
【善心】 (good · heart) .... mercy

Street Hanzi

★ 汉英词汇的近源探秘 ＝

《The Approximation Discovery of Chinese-English Vocabulary Derivations》
(The first book advocating that English and Chinese have the same source in remote antiquity)

Chinese · English	word · converge	（of）	near · source	discover · secret
《汉英	词汇	的	近源	探秘》
Chinese-English	Vocabulary	of	approximation derivations	discovery

(☆ This book is the first one advocating that English and Chinese have a same source in remote antiquity.)

Chinese Characters Index

149

Chinese Proverbs Index

Unit 1 【三e 心ds 二o 意ghts】 (three · minds · two · thoughts)
→ have two minds about

【多s 此s 一ne 举n】 (surplus · this · one · action)
→ make an unnecessary move / burn daylight

Unit 2 【暗k 箭w 伤t 人le】 (dark · arrow · hurt · people)
→ mill in the darkness

【量re 力th 而d 行t】 (measure · strength · and · act)
→ do what one is capable of

Unit 3 【口th 是ght 心t 非ng】 (mouth · right · heart · wrong)
→ cry with one eye and laugh with the other

【铁n 证ce 如ke 山n】 (iron · evidence · like · mountain)
→ irrefutable evidence

Unit 4 【鸡n 犬g 不t 宁l】 (chicken · dog · not · tranquil)
→ even the fowls and dogs are not left in peace

【开n 门r 见e 山n】 (open · door · see · mountain)
→ declare one's intention immediately

Unit 5 【大ly 显y 身y 手d】 (greatly · display · body · hand)
→ display one's talents to the full

【滴p 水er 穿ce 石ne】 (drop · water · pierce · stone)
→ constant dropping wears away a stone

Unit 6 【捕tch 风d 捉tch 影w】 (catch · wind · clutch · shadow)
→ chase the wind and clutch at shadows

【乘de 风d 破k 浪ve】 (ride · wind · break · wave)
→ brave the wind and the waves

Unit 7 【归ning 心t 似ke 箭w】 (returning · heart · like · arrow)
→ with one's heart set on speeding home

【目ye 不t 识w 丁be】 (eye · not · know · cube)
→ be totally illiterate

Unit 8 【隔n 墙l 有ve 耳r】 (partition · wall · have · ear)
→ walls have ears

【鹤ne 立d 鸡n 群p】 (crane · stand · chicken · group)
→ a giant among dwarfs

154

Unit 9 【成shed 竹o 在t 胸st】 (accomplished · bamboo · at · chest)
→ have one's cards up one's sleeves / have a well-thought-out plan

【心t 血d 来me 潮de】 (heart · blood · come · tide)
→ be seized by a whim

Unit 10 【如ke 鱼sh 得t 水er】 (like · fish · get · water)
→ feel just like fish in water

Unit 11 【不t 失se 时me 机ce】 (not · lose · time · chance)
→ not to lose the chance / lose no time

【我 行t 我y 素t】 (I · act · my · element)
→ persist in one's old ways no matter what others say /
the dogs bark, but the caravan goes on

Unit 12 【岂w 有ve 此s 理le】 (how · have · this · rule)
→ there is no such rule

【同me 舟t 共er 济s】 (same · boat · together · cross)
→ cross a river in the same boat

Unit 13 【心t 口th 如s 一ne】 (heart · mouth · as · one)
→ say what one thinks

【时me 不t 我s 待t】 (time · not · us · wait)
→ time and waves wait for no man

Unit 14 【兵er 不t 厌te 诈t】 (soldier · not · hate · cheat)
→ All is fair in war.

【将ng 计ck 就l 计ck】 (bring · trick · deal · trick)
→ turn someone's trick against him

Unit 15 【洗sh 耳rs 恭ly 听n】 (wash · ears · respectfully · listen)
→ listen with respectful attention

【听n 天n 由w 命y】 (listen · heaven · follow · destiny)
→ trust to luck

Unit 16 【敬t 而d 远r 之t】 (respect · and · far · it)
→ stand aloof from sb courteously /
the best defense against an bad man is to keep far away

【不t 耻me 下d 问k】 (not · shame · descend · ask)
→ not feel shamed to ask one's subordinate

Unit 17 【先t 入er 为e 主n】(first · enter · be · main)
→ first impressions are strongest

【齐n 心ts 协t 力ers】(even · hearts · joint · powers)
→ pull all together

Unit 18 【大t 器l 晚te 成te】(great · vessel · late · complete)
→ a great man will take time to shape and mature

【刀d 山ns 火re 海as】(sword · mountains · fire · seas)
→ a mountain of swords and a sea of flame / most severe trial

Unit 19 【断t 章er 取ke 义ng】(cut · chapter · take · meaning)
→ make a deliberate misinterpretation out of context

【迫ch 在t 眉w 睫sh】(approach · at · brow · eyelash)
→ of the utmost urgency

Unit 20 【力th 不t 从w 心t】(strength · not · follow · heart)
→ one's ambition far exceeds one's power

【日ly 理le 万d 机rs】(daily · handle · ten-thousand · affairs)
→ be busy with myriad of affairs

Unit 21 【百d 年rs 大ge 计me】(hundred · years · large · scheme)
→ a hundred years plan

【守d 口th 如ke 瓶le】(guard · mouth · like · bottle)
→ keep one's mouth closed

Unit 22 【本t 性er 难t 移ve】(root · character · difficult · move)
→ be difficult to alter one's character

【千d 载rs 难t 逢t】(thousand · years · difficult · meet)
→ a very rare oppotunity

Unit 23 【恩r 将ng 仇y 报y】(favor · bring · enmity · repay)
→ return evil for good

【深ly 入er 人le's 心ts】(deeply · enter · people,s · hearts)
→ take deep root in the minds of the people

Unit 24 【不t 露l 声ce 色ce】(not · reveal · voice · countenance)
→ not show one's feelings / keep one's countenance

【眉ws 飞y 色ce 舞ce】(eyebrows · fly · countenance · dance)
→ beam with joy / in glee

156

Unit 25 【不t 识w 时t 务r】(not · know · current · affair)
→ show no understanding of the times

【视k 死th 如s 归n】(look · death · as · return)
→ face death unflinchingly

Unit 26 【不o 了d 了d 之t】(no · end · end · it)
→ end up with nothing definite

【饥y 不t 择se 食d】(hungry · not · choose · food)
→ Nothing tastes bad to a hungry man.

Unit 27 【风d 吹w 草s 动ve】(wind · blow · grass · move)
→ be sensitive to a slight upset

【屈d 指ers 可n 数t】(bend · fingers · can · count)
→ can be counted on one's fingers / very few

Unit 28 【吹f 毛r 求k 疵t】(puff · hair · seek · fault)
→ go out of the way to find out faults

【节t 外t 生w 枝ch】(joint · out · grow · branch)
→ side issues crop up unexpectedly

Unit 29 【半f 信ve 半f 疑t】(half · believe · half · doubt)
→ half-believing, half-doubting

【本t 末p 倒t 置ce】(root · top · invert · place)
→ to put the cart before the horse

Unit 30 【原l 形pe 毕ly 露l】(original · shape · wholly · reveal)
→ unmask oneself

【心t 怀t 鬼t 胎s】(heart · pregnant · ghost · fetus)
→ with one's axe to grind

Unit 31 【当le 机ce 立d 断n】(while · chance · stand · decision)
→ prompt a decision at the right moment

【高ly 谈k 阔ly 论s】(highly · talk · widely · discuss)
→ high-flown talk / indulge in loud and empty talk

Unit 32 【成me 千d 上p 万d】(become · thousand · up · ten-thousand)
→ thousands upon thousands

【火re 上ve 浇r 油l】(fire · above · pour · oil)
→ put oil on the fire

Unit 33 【口th 蜜y 腹y 剑d】(mouth・honey・belly・sword)
→ velvet paws hide sharp claws

【水er 深p 火re 热t】(water・deep・fire・hot)
→ hell on earth

Unit 34 【付y 之t 一 笑gh】(pay・it・a・laugh)
→ afford to laugh at / laugh away

【昙m 花er 一ne 现ce】(epiphyllum・flower・one・appearance)
→ remain on the scene for only a brief period

Unit 35 【拔l 苗ng 助p 长w】(pull・seedling・help・grow)
→ pull up seedlings in a vain hope of helping them grow

【提t 心t 吊ng 胆l】(lift・heart・hang・gall)
→ have one's heart in one's mouth

Q&A

Q: *What is a description of the content?*

A: Most people who travel in China do not have the time or interest to tackle the task of learning Chinese language. Using English sentences with key words written in Chinese characters, this book offers a novel approach for English speakers to recognize Chinese characters. So they can catch the meaning of the signs or maps in Chinese streets and feel the trip more interesting.

Q: *What your book is about?*

A: The purpose of this book is not for those who wish to study Chinese speaking and pronunciation. Instead, it provides a fun and easy way to visually recognize Chinese pictograms using common English words and phrases. This unique manner in which the characters are presented, embedded within the English text, provides the learner with a most efficient way of recognizing, on sight, the meaning of the characters.

Q: *Number of components and approximate length of each component?*

A: This book consists of 160 pages divided into 35 units. Specially designed for self-study as well as for easy reference, it introduces over 800 commonly used Chinese characters.

Q: *Nature of the exercises?*

A: Using English phrases written in Chinese characters the reader can read in English and recognize the meaning of the Chinese characters again and again.

Q: *Source of reading passages?*

A: Humor stories, English poems and Chinese ancient poems translated in English.

Q: *Description and number of illustrations?*

A: 35illustrations are used in the textbook showing 35 Chinese character's history.

Q: *A rationale for the publication of the text. Please explain the goal you hope your book will achieve?*

A: Lately, the number of Europeans and Americans visiting China or Japan has swollen to a million or more per year. Most of these visitors have no idea of the meaning of the Chinese characters they see all around them. This is a pity, for to understand a country's language is to understand a country's culture. Most people who visit China or Japan do not have the time or interest to tackle the task of learning thousands of Chinese characters. Using English sentences with key words written in Chinese characters, this book offers a novel approach for English speakers to recognize Chinese characters. A person does not have to know the Chinese or Japanese language, even picking up a few will enhance his or her visit to China or even Japan. The unique manner for the Chinese character studying make this very differently from other Chinese language textbook. Any English speaker who has interest in China or Japan or their cultures will use this book.

Q: *An estimate and description of the potential audience for your book?*

A: I think this book is very useful for the students who study Chinese or Japanese (their languages or cultures), very useful for the businessmen relative to the Chinese or Japanese business and very use for the visitors to China or Japan. So it can offer not only the academic peoples and also the common peoples a good chance to know Chinese characters very easily (without learning Chinese pronunciations or language expressions). The potential audience for this book, I think it maybe hundred thousands to millions every years.

The curriculum vitae of Mr. TAN, JIMIN
(also names JIMMY TAN or WATANABE, SAIMIN)

1957	Born in Shanghai, China
1982	Graduated from Fudan University in Shanghai, China (Japanese Culture. Literary Bachelor Degree)
1984	Graduated form East China Normal University (Chinese Linguistics Master Degree)
1987	Finished the research course in Tokyo University of Japan
1987-1997	Worked for a Japanese trading company Nissho Iwai Corp.
1997-now	Teaching Chinese in universities in Tokyo

Jimmy Tan's **Hanzi** · 汉 字
Chinese Character

Tanjimin method

ISBN-13: 978-981-4239-36-3
ISBN-10: 981-4239-36-4

For your learning solutions:
www.cengageasia.com

9789814239363